MY LIFE AND BATTLES

MY LIFE AND BATTLES

By JACK JOHNSON

Edited and Translated by CHRISTOPHER RIVERS

Foreword by GEOFFREY C. WARD

PRAEGER

Westport, Connecticut
London

Library of Congress Cataloging-in-Publication Data

Johnson, Jack, 1878–1946.
  My life and battles / by Jack Johnson ; edited and translated by Christopher Rivers ;
foreword by Geoffrey C. Ward.
     p.   cm.
  Translation and amalgam of the 1914 autobiography Mes combats and autobiographical
articles that originally appeared in La vie au grand air in 1911.
  Includes bibliographical references and index.
  ISBN 978–0–275–99964–3 (alk. paper)
  1. Johnson, Jack, 1878–1946.   2. Boxers (Sports)–United States–Biography.
3. African American boxers–Biography.   I. Rivers, Christopher.   II. Johnson, Jack,
1878–1946. Mes combats.   III. Vie au grand air.   IV. Title.
  GV1132.J7A3   2007
  796.83092—dc22
  [B]   2007028401

British Library Cataloguing in Publication Data is available.

Library of Congress Catalog Card Number: 2007028401
ISBN-13: 978–0–275–99964–3

First published in 2007

Praeger Publishers, 88 Post Road West, Westport, CT 06881
An imprint of Greenwood Publishing Group, Inc.
www.praeger.com

Printed in the United States of America

The paper used in this book complies with the
Permanent Paper Standard issued by the National
Information Standards Organization (Z39.48–1984).

10 9 8 7 6 5 4 3 2 1

For Christopher Miller

Nothing that Fredrick Douglass did, nothing that Booker T. Washington did, nothing that any African-American had done up until that time had the same impact as Jack Johnson's fight against Jim Jeffries on July 4, 1910. It was the most awaited event in the history of African-Americans to that date. Lincoln's Emancipation Proclamation was not done with widespread prior knowledge. Half of black America didn't know it was going to be issued, and even after it was, many African-Americans didn't know about it for weeks. But virtually every black American knew that Johnson versus Jeffries was going to take place. They knew it; they knew what was at stake; and they also knew they could get the results almost immediately because of the advent of the telegraph. And when Johnson won [. . .] it completely destroyed one of the crucial pillars of white supremacy—the idea that the white man was superior in body and mind to all the darker peoples of the earth. That was just not true as far as anybody was concerned anymore, because now a black man held the title symbolic of the world's most physically powerful human being. It had an emotional immediacy that went beyond what Ali, Joe Louis, or even Jackie Robinson did, because it was the first time that anything like that had ever happened.

—Arthur Ashe

Jack Johnson, the first black heavyweight champion, whose reign lasted from 1908 to 1915, was also the first African-American pop culture icon. He was photographed more than any other black man of his day and, indeed, more than most white men. He was written about more as well. [. . .] Not even the most famous race leaders of the day [. . .] could claim anywhere near the attention Johnson received. Not even the most famous black entertainers and artists of the day [. . .] received Johnson's attention. In fact, it would be safe to say that while Johnson was heavyweight champion, he was covered more in the press than all other notable black men combined.

[. . .] He was scandal, he was gossip, he was a public menace for many, a public hero for some, admired and demonized, feared, misunderstood, and ridiculed. Johnson emerged as a major figure in the world of sports at the turn of the century when sports themselves, both collegiate and professional, were becoming a significant force in American cultural life and as the role of black people in sports was changing. Johnson arrived at a time when the machinery of American popular culture, as we know it today, was being put into place.

—Gerald Early

CONTENTS

Foreword by Geoffrey C. Ward   ix
Preface   xiii
Acknowledgments   xvii

Chapter One: I Enter the World   1

Chapter Two: My First Experience in the Ring   5

Chapter Three: The Tragi-Comic Story of a Black Preacher, a Little
    Colored Boy, and a Bottle of Gin   9

Chapter Four: I Arrive in Boston   15

Chapter Five: My Beginnings in the Noble Art   19

Chapter Six: I Go into Politics   25

Chapter Seven: Joe Choynski Teaches Me What a Knockout Is   29

Chapter Eight: I Fight for Beans!   33

Chapter Nine: My Old Friend Sam McVey   39

Chapter Ten: Two Formidable Opponents: Marvin Hart and Sam
    Langford   43

Chapter Eleven: I Make Some New Year's Resolutions   47

Chapter Twelve: I Go to Australia   51

Chapter Thirteen: I Go Kangaroo Hunting   55

Chapter Fourteen: I Meet Up with Bill Lang and Send Old Man
        Fitzsimmons Off to Dreamland   59

Chapter Fifteen: In Pursuit of Tommy Burns   63

Chapter Sixteen: I Am Champion of the World!   69

Chapter Seventeen: I Defend My Title   75

Chapter Eighteen: The Boxer as Man of the World   79

Chapter Nineteen: Stanley Ketchel's Terrific Right!   85

Chapter Twenty: Mr. Jeffries' Pretensions   89

Chapter Twenty-One: The Fight of My Life   93

Chapter Twenty-Two: Who Will Be the Winner?   97

Chapter Twenty-Three: I Begin Training   101

Chapter Twenty-Four: I Set up Camp in Reno   105

Chapter Twenty-Five: The End of Mr. J. J. Jeffries   109

Epilogue   113

Appendix 1: Advertisement from La Vie au Grand Air *for the
    Serialized Johnson Memoir (January 1911)*   115

*Appendix 2: Chronology of the Life and Battles of Jack Johnson
    (up to 1915)*   117

Notes   123

FOREWORD

Jack Johnson loved to be photographed, in part, I think, because the camera did not caricature him as the racist sportswriters and newspaper cartoonists of his day routinely did. The lens could not be made to lie. Thousands of pictures—snapshots taken on the street as well as formal studio portraits—prove him in his prime to have been almost as handsome, charismatic, and elegantly turned out as he thought he was.

But one photograph, made late in his life, may be the most revealing. He is an old man in the picture. His shaven head and big hands now seem outsized, and his clothes are a little shabby, evidence that he has fallen on hard times. But he is holding his battered scrapbook across his knees, its big pages crowded with clippings about himself, and his grin as he pores over them is rapturous.

Johnson was persuaded from boyhood that he was someone special. He "wasn't figuring on being president," his mother remembered his telling her when he was still a small boy, but "he expects he'll be something what'll be just about as big." And he determined early on that the whole world should be made aware of it. No man ever tended his own legend more assiduously than Jack Johnson did—and "legend" is the operative word. His autobiographical writings—two published memoirs, extensive notes for an unpublished one, and countless newspaper and magazine tellings and retellings of his own story—are filled with exaggerations, embellishments, and outright inventions.

For the record: the story of the hard-drinking pastor told in Chapter Three of this first memoir is almost surely a vaudeville tale having nothing to do with the champion's own life; he was at least sixteen when he left Galveston for Boston, not eleven; he claims to have been married several years before he really was; and he sometimes misstates his own record in the ring, leaving out the fact that middleweight champion Stanley Ketchel managed to knock him down before being felled himself, for example, and fabricating a knockdown by Sam Langford, who was a great favorite with the French public, perhaps in the hope of drumming up a second fight in Paris with the younger, smaller man. (If that was his motive he quickly thought better of it; they would never fight again.)

None of this should be surprising. Veracity and the fight game haven't traditionally had much to do with one another. And the contradictory versions of Johnson peddled by white newspapermen—that he was at once timid and savage, shiftless and overambitious, childlike and deeply corrupt—were themselves colossal lies that he tried hard all his life to offset.

Professor Rivers has performed a real service in translating into English the champion's earliest attempt at self-defense in print. It presents a portrait of Johnson as he himself wished to be portrayed and, for the most part, as he then really was: intelligent, proud, supremely gifted, in control, and at the top of his game.

Was he lazy because he sometimes failed to go for the knockouts others sought? No, he writes, he thought it best always to hold "a little something back," so that no one could ever take his "full measure."

Was he "a yellow nigger" because he preferred to pick his opponents apart rather than mix it up? No, he was a fistic scholar: "The folks who came to see me in the ring thought I was there to hit, to do damage and to take my opponent out. No one would have thought that this big, poor nigger was in the process of methodically learning his craft, with the firm intention of increasing, little by little and through a tough form of education, his knowledge of the sport of boxing. I followed the plan I had set out for myself, without worrying about criticism from people who preferred to think I was an animal without intelligence. . . . "

Was he "uppity," as so many writers said, unwilling to stay where he belonged? Not at all. In sixteen years in boxing, he writes, referring to himself in the third person as he often did, "I couldn't remember a single occasion when Jack Johnson had tried to take a seat that hadn't been offered to him or force his way into a group of whites."

Had a desire for racial revenge motivated him when he took the heavyweight title from Tommy Burns or defended it against Jim Jeffries? Never. In both cases, it had been a question of personal "honor," not race, which drove him to victory. Burns had implied he was a coward and therefore had to be made to eat his words; Jeffries made the same mistake and so suffered the same righteous punishment.

There isn't a hint in this memoir that the chorus of racial epithets that greeted him whenever he entered the arena against a white opponent, or the drum roll of death threats that punctuated his life outside the ring, ever bothered him for a moment. Such things, he wanted his readers to believe, were beneath his notice.

But when *Mes Combats* was published in France in 1914 it must have been hard even for him to keep up that brave front. By then, he had been a fugitive from his own country for months, the victim of a racially motivated federal prosecution for a crime he had not committed. He would spend seven years in exile, lose his title, and serve another year in the federal penitentiary at Leavenworth before finally being allowed to resume what was left of his boxing career at the age of forty-three. Through it all, as his third wife said at his death in 1946, he somehow managed to hold on to both his pride and his courage. "He faced the world unafraid," she said at his graveside. "There wasn't anybody or anything he feared."

—Geoffrey C. Ward

PREFACE

I learned the improbable fact that Jack Johnson's first autobiography was written in French in Geoffrey Ward's masterful biography, *Unforgivable Blackness: The Rise and Fall of Jack Johnson* (New York: Knopf, 2004). *Mes Combats*, published in Paris as a book in 1914, was in fact an abridged version of a series of articles that had appeared in the popular French sports magazine *La Vie au Grand Air* in eighteen consecutive weekly instalments in the first half of 1911, entitled *Ma Vie et mes combats* (*My Life and Battles*).[1]

The text here is an amalgam of the *Vie au Grand Air* articles and the 1914 book. While virtually everything in the 1914 book had already appeared in the articles, quite a lot of the material in the articles was not included in the book. The first few chapters, for example, describing Johnson's boyhood, are not included in the 1914 text, nor are, among other things, the descriptions of Johnson's brief and amusing career as a local politician in Galveston, Texas, his experience hunting kangaroo in Australia, and his epic bouts of seasickness. Interestingly, some of the most explicit commentary on Johnson's part about race and "the color line" in boxing and society at large was left out of the book version as well. It is interesting to speculate about what may have motivated this excision, particularly in light of the fact that the 1911 articles appeared before Johnson's conviction in the United States on trumped-up racist charges and subsequent exile in Europe, while the 1914 book was published during that exile.

None of this material has ever before been translated into English and it presents great interest for any reader interested in Jack Johnson. Like Johnson's famous 1927 autobiography, *Jack Johnson: In the Ring and Out*, the memoir is not always an entirely factually accurate account of the events of Johnson's life and career. It is, however, a fascinating piece of self-mythologizing that provides substantial insights into how Johnson perceived himself and wished to be perceived by others. And as is the case of the 1927 autobiography, Johnson's personal voice comes through clearly—sassy, clever, and invariably charming.

This is remarkable in the case of the French memoir, since Johnson is certainly speaking through a ghostwriter/translator. My guess, from studying the text closely, is that Johnson either wrote or dictated in English and his comments were more or less accurately translated into French. Johnson did speak French, but we don't know how well and it is unlikely that in 1914 his knowledge of French would have been such that writing a book in the language would have been feasible. And there are a few telltale signs that the French is in fact a translation of some oral or written English text, notably the literal translation into French of American-English idioms, resulting in expressions that make sense in French but are not in fact standard French idioms. A few examples: *il était aussi décontenancé qu'une poule sous une averse* ("he was madder than a wet hen"); *déposez-les ou taisez-vous* ("put up or shut up"); *tous mes dollars que j'ai si péniblement gagnés* ("all my hard-earned money"); and *je parierais bien tous les dollars qu'on voudrait contre un morceau de pain d'épices* ("I would bet dollars to doughnuts").

My aim in this translation has been to create a text that flows smoothly and can be read easily by contemporary readers, while retaining a clear sense of the language of the era in which it was written and of Johnson's own verbal style. That style, unmistakable even in French translation, alternates between an often jocular colloquialism and a somewhat flowery formality and is strikingly consistent with that of *Jack Johnson: In the Ring and Out*.

I have maintained for the most part the paragraph structure of the French text, even in cases where it seems a bit odd, in order to maintain the rhythm of the original. In a number of instances, I have corrected misspellings of American names ("Kid Conroy" for example, had somehow become "Kid Comoy," perhaps another indication that Johnson spoke while a nonnative speaker of English transcribed his words). The word *science* appears often in the text; in some contexts I have translated this as "skill" or "skills" and in others as "knowledge." In order to maintain the dual usage in the French, I tried to be consistent in translating *rencontre* as "fight" and *combat* as "bout" (*match* obviously remained "match"). I translated *se mesurer avec* as "square off with."

The chapter divisions differ quite a bit between the *Vie au Grand Air* version and the 1914 book version. I have chosen those divisions that seemed to make the most sense. Most of the chapter titles here are those used in the 1914 text, as they are shorter and more to the point. In cases of entire chapters that exist only in the 1911 version, I have shortened and simplified the titles as necessary. Because of the fact that this translation is an amalgam of the two French versions, the numbering of the chapters does not correspond exactly to that of either of the two. The final chapter of the 1911 text, a brief account of Johnson's homecoming in Chicago after his victory over Jeffries, seemed to me much more appropriate as an epilogue rather than a chapter, thereby allowing the main body of the book itself to end on the dramatic note that serves as the conclusion of the 1914 text ("The last hope of the white race had failed. Since that day, not another has been found to try to replace him.").

The French word *nègre* poses a very particular problem for a translator. It does not carry quite the same hate-filled weight as the word "nigger," accurately characterized by the 2000 edition of the *Random House Webster's College Dictionary* as "probably the most offensive word in English." On the other hand, in 1911, it was a very clearly pejorative and offensive, if commonly accepted, term in French, meaning that there is a definite, if a bit rough, correspondence, between it and the word "nigger." Other possible translations are simply farther off the mark. *Nègre* clearly expressed neither the putative neutrality nor the relative formality of the English word "negro" (which may have been less likely to be used in the kind of colloquial discourse that comprises much, though not all, of this memoir), so that would not be an appropriate choice as translation. Neither would "black," since it translates the word *noir*. The archaic term "colored," in common usage in early twentieth-century America, corresponds to the term *de couleur* but not to *nègre*.

In fact, Johnson's French memoir uses, at various moments and in various contexts, all of these terms. Ultimately, in order to maintain in the translation the distinctions in tone and substance made in the original French, and no doubt in Johnson's original English of which it is a translation, I have maintained the literal correspondences outlined in the preceding paragraph (*noir* = "black"; *de couleur* = "colored"; *nègre* = "nigger"). I have chosen to translate *négrillon*, which is used when Johnson is referring to himself and his childhood playmates, as "little colored boy." The relative "softness" of that term corresponds to the fondness and humor of the tone at those moments and the archaism "colored" seems appropriate in that context.

It is important to note that the term *nègre* is used in a range of different ways here, with a range of affective connotations. At least once *nègre* is used in a clearly nonhostile reference to a fellow black boxer for whom Johnson has great respect (Sam Langford).

Nègre is also used, however, in at least two cases, as part of a direct quotation of anonymous racist jeering at Johnson in the ring. At one point, Johnson imagines the kind of stories his rival Tommy Burns is going around telling about him and puts, no doubt accurately, the hateful word in Burns' mouth (*Tous les boxeurs nègres sont de cette trempe*/"All the nigger boxers are of that caliber").

The most frequent usage of the word, however, occurs in instances of free indirect discourse in which Johnson is not directly quoting a racist epithet but rather channeling racist sentiments that he knows are being directed at him or other black boxers (*Peter Jackson avait bien lancé un défi à John L. Sullivan, mais celui-ci ne voulut pas consentir à se rencontrer avec un nègre*/"Peter Jackson issued a challenge to John L. Sullivan, but Sullivan wouldn't consent to fight a nigger").

An endeavor such as this is necessarily approximate. This translation is my best effort to reconstruct what Johnson's actual English words would have been.

ACKNOWLEDGMENTS

Geoffrey Ward's biography of Jack Johnson, *Unforgivable Blackness*, was the springboard for this project and served as an inspiration in more ways than one. Geoff was kind enough to respond with great enthusiasm and collegiality to an e-mail from a total stranger and then read and respond to the manuscript. Even more impressive is the fact that he agreed to write a foreword and stuck with me for every step of the long and complicated process of finding a publisher. He was unfailingly gracious and his dedication to helping make my project a reality was unwavering. My debt to him is enormous.

Joyce Carol Oates and Randy Roberts were kind enough to read the manuscript and take interest in it, for which I am sincerely grateful.

Gretchen Busl, my former student at Mount Holyoke and currently a student in the PhD in Literature program at Notre Dame, provided the enormous service of going to the rare book collection at Notre Dame and photocopying the page from Jim Jeffries' autobiography that is quoted by Johnson, meaning that I did not have to translate a translation but could use the actual source (without having to make a trip to South Bend).

The staff of Beinecke Library at Yale made the process of obtaining two of the three illustrations in this book extremely easy. Those two photographs come from *Le Champion du monde Jack Johnson*, a rare booklet published in Paris in 1911 by Léon Sée, editor of the magazine *La Boxe et les Boxeurs*; the work is part of the remarkable collection of books and pamphlets related to boxing given to Yale by Herbert Lazarus (Yale '27) and housed at Beinecke

Library. I am also grateful to the staff at Widener Library at Harvard, particularly the librarians in the Phillips Reading Room, for their help.

The time-consuming final stages of getting the book together took place while I was on sabbatical, so thanks are due to Mount Holyoke College as well.

It has been my pleasure to work with terrific people at Greenwood/Praeger, all of whom have been courteous and efficient and have taken a genuine interest in this book. I would like to thank each of them for her/his hard work: Elizabeth Demers, Elizabeth Potenza, Bridget Austiguy-Preschel, Dan Harmon, Navdeep Singh, Anoop Chaturvedi, Himanshu Abrol, Erin Ryan and Celeste Bilyard.

It is no exaggeration to say that Kirik Jenness taught me everything I know about the manly art. He was generous enough to read a draft of the manuscript and to bat around a number of technical and semantic questions with me as I tinkered with the translation. His indefatigable enthusiasm, both for this project and for the less-than-thrilling task of putting on the gloves every Thursday afternoon for years on end with an unskilled, unathletic, middle-aged novice, is awe-inspiring.

Christopher Miller helped in every possible way with each step of the process. He encouraged me to undertake this project from the moment the idea occurred to me and was an excellent proofreader. Perhaps most important, he was a tireless sounding board for an endless stream of obsessive discourse about the project over a period of several years. He provided, as always, both expertise of the highest caliber and support of limitless depth and breadth.

—Christopher Rivers, Editor and Translator

Le champion du monde

JACK JOHNSON

Jack Johnson, champion du monde (from Léon Sée, *Le Champion du monde Jack Johnson* [Paris: Imprimerie Paul Dupont, 1910]) (Herbert B. Lazarus Collection, Beinecke Rare Book and Manuscript Library, Yale University).

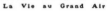
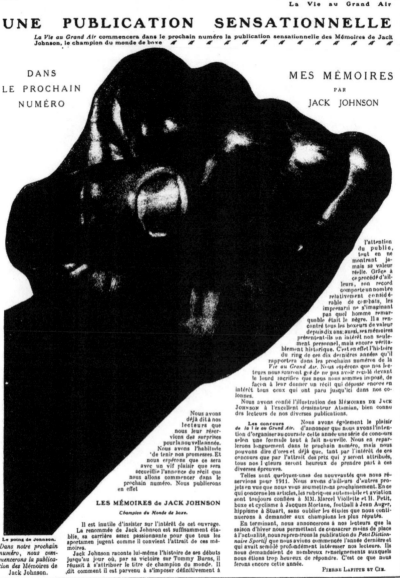

Advertisement from *La Vie au Grand Air* (1910) for Johnson memoir, to be published in serial installments (courtesy of Geoffrey Ward). (See Appendix 1 for translation of text.)

Le célèbre **Bill Jordan**, le speaker de tous les grands combats, présente **Johnson**.

La présentation de Jeffries.

Johnson and Jeffries introduced to the crowd (July 4, 1910). (from Léon Sée, *Le Champion du monde Jack Johnson* [Paris: Imprimerie Paul Dupont, 1910]) (Herbert B. Lazarus Collection, Beinecke Rare Book and Manuscript Library, Yale University).

One

I ENTER THE WORLD

When a white man writes his memoirs, as I am going to try to do here, he tends to begin with the history of his family, going back to the most distant times. The idea seems to be that the farther back he goes, the more interesting his story will be. Consequently, I believe, all authors embellish without hesitation on their genealogy. The fact is, that sort of thing is of interest only to members of the family. On the other hand, I don't wish to avoid participating in such an old custom, so I too will say a few words about my genealogy.

Our memories are transmitted mostly by word of mouth, from father to son. White people can't imagine that we too are proud of our ancestors and that for long days, and even longer nights, when we knew nothing of schools or books, we handed down memories of past centuries. The tales were no doubt modified over time, but the salient facts remained the same. Fable or tradition, it matters little. Can anyone tell me, in the history of a white family over two or three centuries, how much is truth and how much fable?

My father and mother, and many generations of their forebears before them, lived in North Carolina. If I had to establish my pedigree, I could say that my ancestors arrived in North America with the first white colonists. If one had to prove long residence in order to be granted full rights and privileges in this country, I could boast of being a purebred American, as we settled in this country with the exiles from Monmouth's Revolt in England, 150 years before anyone had even dreamed of the United States.

You white men are mighty proud when you can trace your lineage back to the Crusades, something like ten centuries ago. But can you tell me who built those edifices that your ancestors found in Palestine at the time of the Crusades, already twenty centuries old at the time? To what country did Solomon go, seeking the gold to cover the roof of his temple? Who built the pyramids forty centuries ago? Which race erected the monuments of Egypt, before anyone knew Europe even existed—when the inhabitants of Europe, dressed in animal skins, were still scraping out a miserable existence in caves? Who? But what good does it do to ask such questions? I took up the pen to talk only of things of our own era.

What I know for sure is that it is to this long line of ancestors, all of them hard workers, people who lived in the open air, that I owe my size, the strength of my arms, and the quality of my muscles, all qualities that make up a heritage of which I am as proud as others might be of a baronet's coat of arms.

While still young, my parents emigrated from Carolina to Texas. This was at the time of the Lone Star Republic. Texas was fighting Mexico for its independence and the poor inhabitants of the border led a very hard life, able to work in the fields only between skirmishes with the Indians and the Mexicans.

Then came the Civil War, in which my father fought from beginning to end. He was at the Siege of Vicksburg and with Grant at the Battle of Appomattox, which brought an end to the war. Between the two, he took part in numerous battles. My father was one of the strongest men, physically, I have ever known. He wasn't quite as tall as I am, but he was solidly built and very broad through the shoulders. He carried a barrel of sugar or lard with great ease and could lift a 500-pound bale of cotton with one hand. In the army, he was known for his strength. He often gave a hand getting a cannon out of a hole or turning it on its mounting. I believe he would have made a good boxer if he had ever taken that path. He never spoke to me about his military experiences but from some of the conversations that I overheard him have with his friends, I learned that he was often called on to straighten out the hotheads of his regiment.

After the war, he returned to his parents, got married, and set himself up in Galveston, where I was born, thirty-three years ago. The hard work he did in the army had disturbed his robust condition and he got a job as a cleaning man in one of the big houses in town.

As for me, I spent the days of my early childhood like all children of my race and condition did: running in the street, playing hooky from school as often as possible, and strolling along the port looking at the boats.

But as soon as I was old enough to work, that was the end of loafing around. There were six children at home to be fed and clothed. My mother had given birth to nine, but three of them died before I was born. So there were some hard times in our little house in Galveston, and as soon as I was big enough, my father took me on as his helper, as his work as a cleaning man kept him very busy. There was no such thing as a carpet sweeper or a vacuum cleaner in those days. There were only old-fashioned brooms, with which I did the sweeping. Those damn brooms were bigger than I was and one of my greatest moments was when I grew to be as tall as the handle. But I do believe that it was handling a broom from the time I was a young child that strengthened my back and shoulder muscles. I point out this training method for what it's worth.

The first money I earned was from a milkman who had many customers in Galveston. He gave me the job of taking care of his horse while he delivered the bottles of milk. Soon he was the one who stayed in the car while I went up and down, staircase after staircase. Every Saturday night, he gave me ten cents and a pair of red socks. Those were my week's wages. I always wondered where he got all those red socks. And I was plenty proud of them too, but not as proud as I was of my ten cents.

The first fight of my life is still fresh in my memory. My parents were very pious, God-fearing people, and members of the Methodist church. No one was more insistent that their children always stay on the straight-and-narrow. I had never gotten in a fight and never even wondered whether I would dare risk such a thing.

Near our house, there was a black kid by the name of Jackie Morris who was the true tyrant of the neighborhood. All the other children, boys as well as girls, had to obey his rules. Since I was already big for my age, he went out of his way to tease me, to pinch me, and to torment me in a thousand different ways when he met up with me. I didn't realize that I was capable of giving him a beating and so I ran away when I saw him.

Right across the street lived an old black woman we all called Grandma Gilmore. One day she called me over and said: "Listen, Jack, the next time that Morris boy bothers you, you give him a good punch and he'll leave you alone. Understand?"

As it happened, that very same day Jackie saw me and started running after me, like always. I stopped and waited for him to catch up. When he saw that, he stopped too. That gave me courage. I jumped on him; I had months and months' worth of persecution to avenge. I got my revenge and then some. After that, when we met in the street I wasn't the one who ran away.

But for the whole rest of the day, I was much more scared than I had been in the fight. My mother called me to her. She looked completely indignant but all she did was make me sit down next to her. When she had finished reading a chapter from the Bible, she simply said: "I'm going to tell your father when he comes home."

My father got home. We sat down to dinner and as soon as he had lifted his head from saying grace, my mother said: "Do you know what our little wretch Jack did today? He got into a fight!"

"A fight!" said my father, slowly lifting his eyes from his plate. "With who?"

"With Jackie Morris."

My father looked at me with a smile masquerading as a grimace and said: "Yes, I saw Jackie this evening in his yard when I passed by his house. He did look like to me like he had taken a beating."

That was all and so I began to breathe more easily. After that day, I often had animated disputes with boys who were older and bigger than I was and my father never paid any attention to it. If I had a son, I would certainly not want him to spend his time fighting. But if he were attacked and didn't give the attacker a beating in return, I would be the one to beat him when he came home. Fights between kids give them self-confidence and are the first lesson in the struggle for survival.

Two

MY FIRST EXPERIENCE IN THE RING

The only spectators at my first public fight were some brats of my own age standing around in a circle. That was nonetheless when I had my first experience of the ring and tasted for the first time the sweetness of encouragements and the joy of triumph. The man at the origin of the dispute was a policeman.

I had just gotten to that age where a boy takes great pride in being able to play with boys older and bigger than he is. Mooning around the docks and in the streets, I had often stopped to watch the big boys throw dice in the shadow of a bale of cotton or behind some warehouse. It didn't take me long to learn how to shake those dice and mutter wishes for luck under my breath.

One afternoon—I forget if I was playing or if I was just an enthusiastic spectator—a big policeman came rushing at us out of the blue. The whole gang scattered like a flock of sparrows but I got caught. I could feel the solid grasp of the policeman on the collar of my shirt. He was leading me away when, at the first street corner, we spied another little colored boy, Dave Pearson, lying down in a biscuit crate, moving his bare legs and feet as if he were half-asleep. When he saw me in the policeman's grip, he woke up all of a sudden and looked at us with well-feigned astonishment. I should mention that Dave was in fact one of the keenest participants in the game that had been so unfortunately interrupted. But when the policeman rushed at me, Dave, who was older and had long legs, had been able to run away without being noticed. He went around the block and stuffed himself in a crate, where he now sat looking like an innocent black cherub.

The policeman didn't say anything and I was careful not to breathe a word, but when we got up next to the crate, he stopped and looked at Dave straight in the face. That was enough; the innocent cherub was transformed into a terrified little colored boy. He leapt out of his crate to run away. But his bare feet hadn't even touched the ground before he got nabbed. He had made a mistake. If he had stayed calm, the policeman would have passed right by him without a word.

"So I've got you, too, you little wretch," he said, as he proceeded to parade down the street with a colored boy in each hand, both of them looking sheepish and like they would rather be somewhere else. A little later, our mothers came to get us, promising to punish us as soon as they got us home.

The rumor started that I was the one who had denounced Dave to the policeman. This was a lie and one of those offenses that can't be forgiven. I was so indignant that I almost went crazy and I used words I had never used in my life.

"That's a damn lie and I'll beat the tar out of the damn liar who said it."

"Suppose it was Dave Pearson himself who said it," another kid said.

"I don't care if it was the devil himself, I'm not backing down!"

The next day, I ran into Dave on the docks.

"Are you the one who said I was a damn liar?"

"I said that anyone who said I turned him in was a damn liar and that I would beat the tar out of him."

"Out of me?"

"Yes, out of you, if you're the one who said it!"

We didn't say another word and immediately the gang of kids formed a circle around us. Dave was older and heavier, and he had more experience. But I fought like a madman and ended up getting the better of him.

After that, I had a number of disputes with other boys, for trivial matters that seemed very important to us. Sometimes it had to do with a nickel, sometimes with an argument between the two of us. Anyone who remembers his childhood knows that in a group of kids, there are always battles going on. But I can say that while I never avoided a fight, I never sought one out either and that I never punched kids who were younger and weaker. Consequently, I was liked by everyone.

To go back farther in my memory, I recall that at the age of nine, I was already looking for ways to earn my living. I was not content pushing a broom behind my father; I wanted to get out and work on my own.

As I said, life was not easy in our little house in Galveston and the days when our stomachs were empty were more numerous than the feast days. My mother often had worries and I tried to console her.

"Just wait, Mama," I would tell her. "When I grow up, I'm going to buy a lot and build a two-story house, with a balcony all around it and plants climbing all over it. And out back, we'll have a yard, where we'll have a cow and some chickens that will lay beautiful eggs for you."

And then I'd ask her to let me go, telling her that I would surely come back with some money. But she just made fun of me and said that all I had to do for the time being was go to school and learn how to be an honest man.

But this was an *idée fixe* for me, to leave my parents' house to earn money. With this constant preoccupation, I ran away from home several times. But each time, my sister Lucy managed to find me and bring me back home. It was only the last time that I managed to get away from her. Sometimes she pulled me home by the ear; other times, she had to drag me. Good old sister Lucy! She liked me and I know she had only my best interest in mind.

My mother, like all the good mothers I have known, had too soft a heart. She had a whole nest full of impossible children, but she was incapable of punishing them. When we saw her pick up a switch, we would pretend to fall down and start sniffling; instead of the switch, she would end up giving us a piece of cake.

With sister Lucy, on the other hand, things were different. She knew all my tricks, since she had used them herself. There was no way to pull the wool over her eyes. Unlike my mother, she wouldn't hesitate to pick up a whip and whip us with it.

I did my best to resist her, but she was a strapping young woman and stronger than me. I always said that I hadn't done anything but now I admit that when she punished me, it was because I deserved it.

There was one thing I loved more than anything else in the world and that was bread pudding. I always prowled around the oven the day my mother was making some. All children love food but this was especially true of me. I couldn't wait until the treat was done and the minute my mother turned her back, I would open the oven and cut off a little piece. If I didn't have a knife or spoon handy, I would use my fingers. Sometimes I burned myself terribly, but that didn't matter to me. Sometimes, my sister Lucy would see me. She would rush at me, like a mother hen shooing away her chicks, and it always ended badly for me.

No matter what method I used to run away, Lucy always managed to find me. If I hid in a train, planning to get off at the next station, she would find out about it and come get me. If I ran away to the harbor, I didn't even have time to decide which warehouse I was going to move into or which crate would be my home before Lucy was there, before nightfall. She really was a witch of some kind!

Nonetheless, the last time I left home, I found a way that made it impossible for Lucy to follow me. But before I tell that story, I should tell you the reasons for my little escapade. The story I am going to tell you is already well-known, but I want to tell it to you the way it really happened. It didn't seem quite so funny when it happened to me. In fact, it seemed utterly tragic to me at the time, but now I realize that it was a joke.

Three

THE TRAGI-COMIC STORY OF A BLACK PREACHER, A LITTLE COLORED BOY, AND A BOTTLE OF GIN

The three main characters of the story that I now know to be a comedy but which struck me at the time as an impressive tragedy are a black preacher, whom we will call Simons (not his real name but he is still living and a God-fearing man and I would not want to offend his beliefs nor reopen an old wound), a bartender named Paul and a little colored boy not quite twelve years old, whose name I don't need to remind anyone of. Before beginning this tale, I should remind my readers that my parents were both very pious and among the most dutiful members of the Methodist church.

Brother Simons was the pastor of a little church where he gave the sermon every Sunday. During the week, he exercised the profession of laundry-man, as well as several other more or less strange occupations, in order to add to the emoluments he earned as a preacher. He was a good laundry-man; but it didn't take long for those who hired his services to notice that a bit of gin, "for the stomach," was his preferred sin. Consequently, when they brought their laundry to him, they made sure to add a little black bottle and the work went all the better for it. When you heard him singing the hymn, "What Will You Do When the Great Day Comes?" you knew that there was no need to worry about him and that his work would be done quickly and done well.

This is what happened the Saturday in question. That day, good old Simons had gotten a big basket of laundry to do and a bottle of proportionate size. When evening came, he felt very tired, his mouth was dry, and he told himself that a big glass of gin would do his stomach some good. So he called the little colored boy over.

"Say, Jacky," he said, "Why don't you go over to Paul's house with this bottle and tell him to put a half-pint of gin in it for me. Tell him I'll pay him next week."

Those readers who have had the experience of drinking a certain amount of gin in an evening can easily imagine how our upstanding pastor felt on Sunday morning.

When the time came for church, he wasn't thinking too clearly. He had a reputation for talking a great deal and people thought he had a gift for improvisation. Unfortunately, he had had too much to do the night before to prepare his improvisation. He was sitting on a crate in the sacristy, thinking to himself that if he just had a few little glasses of gin to clear his mind, things would be a whole lot better. Behind the door, on a little shelf, he spied a black bottle. He looked at it out of the corner of his eye and addressed a few friendly smiles in its direction. But it didn't respond, which is not surprising, since it was empty. All of a sudden, he saw, behind the church, the very same little colored boy who had run his errand for him the night before. He called him over and held out the bottle to him: "Here, son, take this bottle and run over to Mister Paul's house. Tell him to pour a pint of gin in it. Brother Simons is feeling a little weak this morning and will be much obliged."

The kid took the bottle and took off running, while the pastor stayed in the sacristy, still thinking about his upcoming sermon.

After a time, the choirmaster started singing a hymn in the church, with all the members of the congregation singing along, but still no boy and still no bottle. The preacher didn't appear; the choirmaster struck up another hymn, and the congregation joined in on the chorus, but the kid still wasn't there.

Realizing that he couldn't put it off any longer, Brother Simons made a desperate attempt to stand up, go into the church, and climb into the pulpit. He set his top hat, which still had some traces of soap on it, down next to him. He threw his handkerchief into his hat, adjusted his glasses, coughed two or three times to clear his throat, and opened the Bible at random. But the words wouldn't come. He hesitated and, glancing at the congregation, who were absorbed in respectful silence, he began:

"Dear brothers and sisters, we will find the subject of our conversation this morning in the words of Saint Paul and Saint Peter. Do you know what those two apostles say? You don't know. What does Paul say? You have no idea." Banging on the pulpit with his fist, he continues:

"And what does Paul say, I ask you again?"

All of a sudden, a child's voice comes from the back of the church.

"He says, sir, that he won't give you any more gin until you pay for last night's bottle."

At that, Brother Simons came tearing down the steps of the pulpit, to the great stupefaction of his audience. I leapt out of the church and ran all the way to the port, with the pastor on my heels. I managed to lose him for a second and hop onto a boat that was casting off at that very moment. I slipped aboard unnoticed amidst the confusion of the departure and managed to hide myself under the ship carpenter's bench. Soon the ship was heading out of the harbor. It was, I have since learned, a steamer called *The Independence*, captained by Sam Bill and on its way to Boston.

I was between eleven and twelve years old at the time. I had often been on boats in the harbor or on the river, but I had never been out to sea. All of sudden, my head started spinning, the bottom dropped out of my stomach, and I began to get sick—you can't imagine how sick. I had just made the acquaintance of seasickness. I stayed hidden there for an entire day, when suddenly a sailor saw me. He grabbed my foot, dragged me out of my hiding place, and took me to the captain. He was a nice man and didn't have it in him to hurt a little kid. He asked me how I had come to be on board his ship.

"What is your name, kid?" he asked.

"Johnny Johnson, sir."

"Where do you live?"

"Galveston, sir."

"What's your father's name?"

"Henry Johnson, sir."

"Where are you headed?"

"Wherever *The Independence* is going, sir."

"You're a rascal!"

And with that he shot a furious look at me. But I was too sick to be afraid of anything. The captain turned to the second mate and said: "Register this kid in the ship's log, along with his father's name and address, and send him to the galley. We'll unload him in Key West."

I thought I was going to Boston. How I would get there, I had do idea. For the moment, I asked only one thing, to feel solid earth beneath my feet. I was too sick to be able to help in the galley in any way. Since I wasn't eating anything, I didn't cost them much.

I spent my time on deck, as far away as possible from the eyes of the officers, for the two or three days before we got to Key West. There I was literally thrown off the steamer and I found myself, a sad and lamentable waif, in an unknown city. I wandered aimlessly for an hour or two, and I saw lots of people of my color going on board ship, offering seashells to the passengers. A little while on firm ground had cured my stomach; I forgot my former illness and decided to try to slip back onto *The Independence*. I strolled along the seashore for a minute and picked up some seashells, no doubt abandoned there by some children. I slipped up the plank with my cargo. I had no sooner put my foot on deck than one of the quartermasters saw me and recognized me. He took off running after me. I threw my seashells down so that I could slip away faster. But what despair I felt when I saw the old *Independence* lift anchor without me!

At that time, there was only one boat per week that went between Boston and Galveston with a stop in Key West. So I was there for at least a week and perhaps more. My three or four days of fasting and seasickness had left me tired and famished. To sleep, all I had to do was lie down somewhere, but eating was another story. I began to seek out what resources were available in the city for a young nigger who wanted to earn his living. But I wasn't the only one in that situation and the only thing I could come up with was to go out on the water with some sponge-fishermen. I already knew how to swim and dive quite well and I wasn't asking for much as far as salary went. I wasn't able to work very long, though, because I immediately fell prey to another bout of that damn seasickness. Nonetheless, since I didn't cost the fishermen much, they kept me on for two or three days; after that, they got tired of the boy who persisted in getting sick and I found myself on the pavement once again.

I walked along the docks and in the streets, always looking to pick up something to eat, sleeping on a bale of cotton or a spool of wire. Finally, I met a stevedore and told him that I wanted to go as far as Boston. He confessed that he was going to try to stow away on the next steamer himself and asked me to go along with him. We hatched an entire plot.

The next day, the steamer arrived. When it had docked, they began by unloading some merchandise in order to load others. This work took place by means of a very primitive plank on which carts were pushed. I helped my new friend in his work. Not surprisingly, no one recognized us among the dozens and dozens of dockworkers coming and going from the deck to the dock and vice versa. I was helping push carts; on the next-to-the-last trip, I simply forgot to go back down to the dock. My comrade brought his last load on aboard and came back one more time to help one of his buddies, who left the ship by himself. Lost amidst the crowd of passengers, no one paid any attention to us and soon we were out at sea. We had brought with us enough provisions for a trip of several days. If it hadn't been for the damn seasickness that hit me again the minute we pulled out of the harbor, I would have made it to Boston without any trouble.

Four

I ARRIVE IN BOSTON

I lay there for about a day, flattened by seasickness, which was made even worse by the nauseating smell that pervaded the little nook where we were hiding. I thought I was going to die; the fact that I didn't die is no doubt because the moans I was unable to stifle attracted the attention of a sailor. A few minutes later, I was hauled out of my hole and dragged up on deck. As soon as I got there, I was brought before the captain and was living through the very same scene that had taken place with Captain Sam on the *Independence*. It ended the same way, too, with my being sent down to the galley to serve as helper to the ship's cook.

The cook gave me a big pot full of potatoes to peel. The heat in the stifling galley and the smell of grease did nothing for the state of my health. As a result, the cook immediately had enough of me and when my potatoes had been peeled, he thanked me and sent me off to the boiler-room to help shovel coal. An eleven-year-old kid, seasick, locked in the boiler-room of a steamship! You get the picture. I didn't have the strength to lift a shovel and the shovelers took pity on me. I spent my time eating lemons. My goodness, I must have swallowed a crate-full, without eating any other food at all. When I arrived in Boston, my gums were in such bad shape and my teeth so sore that I could no longer close my jaw.

Imagine my joy when I was able to set foot on solid ground! True, I didn't have a red cent, I didn't know a soul, and it was the first time I had seen a big city. I also knew from experience how other kids welcome a "newcomer."

My first efforts were to find a bed and enough to eat to regain my strength. I found refuge in the home of a good woman, Mrs. Dibble, who put me to work cleaning her house morning and night and sent me to school in the afternoons. In between, I did odd jobs here and there, to earn a little money. In the end, things went really well for me in Boston. Naturally, I had a number of quarrels with the local boys, who were eager to see what the newcomer was made of. I didn't seek out these confrontations but I didn't run away from them either; as result, they soon left me alone.

The memory of one of those battles in particular has stayed with me. It was with another black boy named Lewis. He was the cock of the walk in the neighborhood; we soon made each other's acquaintance and the result of our conversation was a fight in the public square. This time, it was serious business. He was a West Indian and had some knowledge of boxing. The fight was the toughest I had ever had up to that point. But I really wanted to win in order to maintain my standing with the other boys. The battle continued until some spectators, who had stopped to watch us punch each other, decided that it had gone on long enough and separated us. I admit that I was quite happy about that decision and so was my opponent, although he didn't say so.

I stayed in Boston for about four years, going to school as often as I could. I also worked when I could find something to keep me busy and I carefully set my money aside. Thus I was able, once or twice during those four years, to make the trip to see my parents and spend a few days with them. I got seasick again but this time I paid my way.

I was about fifteen when I left Boston for good, to go home to my parents. I stayed at home for a while, looking for work in Galveston or thereabouts. I finally decided to turn to horseracing. For two years, I was a stable boy, a jockey, and a trainer. At the beginning, I worked in Mr. Moseley's stable but I left after a while and worked for Gayheart, then Joyce, and finally Bob Miller. Miller owned one of the fastest racehorses I've ever ridden. She was a filly named "Miss Susie" and was considered a real phenomenon in Texas.[1]

Naturally, I had a few disputes with associates that ended in the usual fashion. Most of the time, they were about professional matters, the wrong way to ride in a race, the relative merits of our colts, etc. Other times, they were about collecting on bets, which was not always possible without persuasion. But there's no use in going into all that.

I never had a serious accident in a race, but I do remember one that kept us laughing for a few days. I was training a yearling and one morning I rode him bareback. He was a colt with a lot of promise and I wanted to see what he could do. I was galloping at full speed, when suddenly the reins broke. The colt stopped dead in his tracks but I kept going. I flew over his head, landed on the track on my backside, and slid in that position for about twenty yards. The stable boys burst out laughing and said I was going so fast the track behind me was smoking. The fact was, I had no skin left on my backside and could neither ride nor sit nor sleep on my back for several days.

But I was too heavy to be a jockey and had too much trouble making the weight. So I abandoned horses for bicycles. I quickly became very skilled. I won a fair number of races and lost some, too. I was fairly good at the sport, but even if I had persisted in it, I would never have become world champion. I had a rather serious fall one day, in a five-mile race with Clem Johnson, in Galveston. My leg and ribs were seriously injured and I had to be taken to the hospital. That accident led me to give up cycling and look for a less dangerous profession.

I entered into the employ of a housepainter named Walter Lewis, in Dallas. As it happened, this painter was a boxing fan, and I learned more from him about how to land a haymaker than how to paint a window or paper a wall. Almost every evening, we got together in the backroom of his shop; he may not have known much about boxing, but he taught me everything he knew. My endurance and wind increased as a result.

Five

MY BEGINNINGS IN THE NOBLE ART

I started looking for opponents in the area; it was in Galveston that I fought for money for the first time. When you consider the relatively sizeable sums earned by top ranked boxers, you might be led to believe that being a boxer is the ideal career. But for every fighter who breaks through, how many are there who barely manage to scrape out a living? And all of them, champions and journeymen alike, experience hard times at the start. For me, those hard times were terrible. Many times I climbed into the ring without having eaten a thing for twenty-four hours or without anything in my stomach but a little bit of bread and some buttermilk. I assure you that I had to have a vigorous will not to just give up. But I was sustained by the idea that I had to earn money if I wanted to come to the aid of my poor mother, who had a whole brood of children to feed.

So you can imagine the joy I felt when I won my very first victory in my very first fight! It was against an individual by the name of Lee, who was a tough opponent. I finished him off in the sixteenth round, with a right to the body, followed up by a left to the jaw.[1] After that, I fought a few men in and around the Galveston area, then left the area to go to Memphis. I squared off with Klondike, whom I beat in nine rounds. A few years later, I met up with him again and we fought to a draw in twenty rounds. In our last bout, I put him to sleep in the thirteenth round.

I left there for Chicago, but the state of my finances did not allow me to get any farther than Springfield. I joined the stable of an individual by the name of John Carter, who put me up for two weeks before he got me a match. Unable to find a serious opponent for me, he got five—five big rascals that I had to demolish one after the other. They weren't exactly formidable, but I was starting to get really tired by the time I got to number five.

From Springfield, I headed off again, still in the direction of Chicago, where I arrived without a penny to my name. I looked everywhere to set up a match, but there was nothing for me. I was an unknown novice and no one, in a city where everyone is wild about sports, had any money to lose on me. Finally, Frank Childs took me on as one of his sparring partners. I still laugh when I think of that experience. Frank didn't have a dollar to pay me, but he bestowed on me the title of "head trainer," which had a nice ring to it! Since we didn't have enough money to rent two rooms, I slept in the bed with Frank. One night, his wife arrived at the hotel where we were living. It was a winter night. There was a mixture of rain and sleet coming down and the wind was blowing hard off the lake. It was around midnight when she knocked on the door. She was a quarrelsome and very jealous woman.

"Who is it?" Frank asks.

"You know good and well who it is, damn it," she says. "Open this door!"

"Well wait a minute," Frank says, and he poked me with his elbow, thinking that I was asleep.

"You got to shove off, Jack, my wife is here and it doesn't look like she's in a very good mood. Get dressed and take off!"

"For God's sake, Frank, I wouldn't put the neighbor's dog out on a night like this. You know I don't have a penny to my name. If she wants to come in, let me sleep on the floor until morning. At least I'll be out of the rain and the wind."

But he wouldn't hear of it and I had to leave. I didn't have enough in my pocket to pay for a five-cent bed. I spent the rest of the night wandering the streets, in the rain, sometime stopping in a doorway for a bit of shelter until I heard a policeman's footsteps. Then I would start walking again. It would have been pretty pathetic for a trainer to be arrested in those conditions. Around two o'clock in the morning, I was sitting at the foot of the statue of General Logan, next to the lake. I was huddled behind the pedestal, using it as a windbreak. I must have been really tired or maybe I was trembling from the cold, because it seemed like the enormous bronze horse was turning in the wind like a weathervane.[2]

Six years later, I found myself face-to-face with Frank Childs in the ring, in Los Angeles. I was merciless. As I stepped up onto the platform, I said to myself: "So here we are! Mr. Childs, I am going to make you pay for that night you made me spend in the streets of Chicago." And I gave it to him good for a full thirteen rounds, hitting him like a hammer hits an anvil. All around me, I could hear the crowd yelling: "Black brute!" and other insults. The people observing my fury had no idea that I was paying back a debt.

Childs had promised to pay my room and board while I was in training. I ate in a little restaurant run by Walter Brothers. Oh my, the meals that Mr. Walter Brothers served us for twenty-five cents! They were true wonders, but my ability to put them away was a wonder too. Finally, Mr. Brothers told me that if he didn't see a little money coming in, he was going to cut me off. I couldn't hold it against him. He nonetheless agreed to an arrangement whereby I would get one meal a day and I went on like that for a while. But you should have seen my one meal! I sat down to the table at 11:00 and I ate enough to keep me going until the next day: ten or twelve biscuits (they would bring me a whole tray of them), five glasses of sweet milk straight from the dipper, beefsteaks, chops, and absolutely anything else that happened to be on the table. After a few days, though, I had to say goodbye to that once-a-day meal.

I had a room that didn't cost me much, but I couldn't even afford to pay for that. So one night I tied a rope around the handles of my trunk, opened the window and lowered the package to the ground. Then I left the house as quietly as I could, walked around to the side where my window was, picked up my trunk, and left for New York.

This took place around 1896. I decided to go find Scaldy Bill Quinn, who was in training for his fight with Joe Walcott. I asked him to take me on board, but he just laughed in my face and turned his back on me. I was just a poor rascal of a penniless nigger in those days . . . and dying of hunger to boot. Quinn and his sparring partners were living large; they would throw five-dollar bills to the kids, to have them drink to Quinn's victory in his next fight. But there was no five-dollar bill for Jack Johnson. I hung around, hoping that one would come my way and that I could buy myself five dollars' worth of mutton or pork, with some beans and ham and eggs on the side. But nothing came my way and finally I timidly went up to Quinn and asked him for three cents to take the boat. He shot me a furious look and told me not to bother him anymore. I turned around, but I thought to myself: "It doesn't matter, some day *I'll* be champion."

After he got knocked out by Joe Walcott, I didn't see Scaldy Bill until eight or nine years later, in Chicago. I was on a streetcar and he jumped on the running board to ask me for a handout. I said the exact words he had said to me when I asked him for three cents.

"You coldly pushed me aside when I was dying of hunger and fatigue. You refused to give me three cents to take the boat. Why would I give you something now? Get out of here!"

After Scaldy Bill had turned me away, I crossed the river, I don't remember how, and found myself, for better or worse, at Walcott's training camp. Walcott agreed to take me on board; I helped him with his training while he was in Boston and he paid my room and board at the house of a woman named Mrs. Taylor.

"What do you want to eat?" Mrs. Taylor asked me.

"I'm not fussy, ma'am. For lunch, I'll take a whole roast chicken, preferably a Leghorn because they're the fattest. As far as the rest goes, I'll eat whatever you've got on hand, like everyone else."

I got my daily chicken, but when Joe came around to pay the bill, you should have heard him holler. The bill was for $90.

"For God's sake, Jack, I have never eaten as well as you do."

He paid the bill nonetheless and, for my salary, gave me two of his old pieces of clothes. He didn't lose anything on the deal.

At that point, I left Walcott and became the manager of Kid Conroy, a charming boy who had a powerful punch and who could nearly knock me down when we sparred. I won a few fights with him. While I was his manager and trainer, I lived with him at his mother's house, where I was very well treated indeed. I got him into such good shape that he managed to fight Jim Bradley to a draw.

There was a gang of Italians in our neighborhood who sold fruit and liked me a lot. Every day they sent me baskets of the best fruit they had. Morris Hahn, a millionaire and a big sports fan, gave us lots of money; he gave me personally eight or nine suits. Mr. Hahn's disappearance was a very strange thing. Some time after I had left New Haven, he dropped out of sight and since then, as far as I know no one has heard a word about him. Conroy beat all the men in his weight class in the region. Thanks to the arrangements we had made, he earned me more than I could have hoped for.

With the money I had earned as a manager, I went back to Galveston. With the handsome suits Mr. Hahn had given me, I was a real dandy! What an impression I made! I remember having a lot of social success at that point!

Around that time, the city started to seem a bit too familiar to me and I began traveling again. First I left for St. Louis; from there, I started fighting all over the state, in Sedalia and other places, anywhere I could find a match. The purses were quite modest then and I had to be very economical with my money.

All that time, I was studying men, how they behaved in the ring, their physiognomy, learning to read the fear, anxiety, suffering, and discouragement on their faces. I figured out which ones to push and provoke until they went into a rage and which ones to fight calmly. Every man I fought taught me a new lesson. I was still a novice, but I was set in my mind that I would become a champion. For the time being, I wasn't a man yet and it was hard to find someone willing to hire me. Later on, people acquired more confidence in me.

Six

I GO INTO POLITICS

From Missouri, I returned to Chicago. I arrived dead broke, as was my custom. In order to procure the three meals my constitution required, I fought several lightweights and won a few purses. The purses were, unfortunately, too modest but they were nonetheless enough to get me on my feet for a few weeks. Then I left for New York, where I had similar successes. All of this was none too encouraging for a man who had it in his head to become a world champion and have an otter-skin coat and diamond studs in his shirt. In bars, where I couldn't drink, I looked for backers who would agree to launch me in my pugilistic career.

I finally returned to Galveston and decided to go into politics. That may seem like the least likely decision for a man in my situation to make, but the fact was that I didn't see that there was anything better to do at the time.

Besides, I had always thought I would like to try out the business world. So I took off my jacket, rolled up my shirtsleeves and got ready to do the things one did in the new career I had just chosen.

My attempt at politics may not have much usefulness for novices who would like to learn from my example and I would not encourage beginners in the art of boxing to follow it, but it was a very amusing period of my life. I didn't tarry long in the world of political affairs but I put more into the endeavor in those few weeks than do lots of people who devote their entire lives to it. It was one of the most comical adventures of my existence and I still laugh today when I think about it.

The details are not important. Even I don't remember how it came to pass, but what I do know is that I was elected president of the Republican Club of my neighborhood in Galveston. I should point out that there were not many white people in this club, for the good reason that there weren't very many in the neighborhood. When I took my place in the president's seat, I made a little speech. I let it be known that I didn't need anyone to lead the debates and that when I proposed something, I didn't expect there to be any argument about it. If any of my readers wishes more detailed information, all he has to do is contact Galveston, where there are plenty of people who have excellent reasons to remember my brief career as the neighborhood politician. At least several of them can attest to the fact that I had no great trouble maintaining order and that there were few protests against my presidential decisions.

After a while, I ran for election as president of the countywide committee. Don't think for a second that I was the only candidate. There were two factions in the neighborhood and they were more or less equal in number. One evening, I scheduled a committee meeting, during which my candidacy was to be affirmed. Everything was going well, when into the room came a troop of people belonging to the other faction, who were there with the sole purpose of disrupting our meeting. I had taken every precaution to avoid this sort of thing and would have been very disappointed if I hadn't been able to stop it. Their intention was to seize the podium and nominate one of their own. But I was prepared for anything.

The leader of the opposition was a great big fellow by the name of Big Six. He was a coach-driver by profession and his stature allowed him to impose his will on all the members of his faction. There had never been any trouble between us, but the minute I saw him enter the room, leading his troop, I knew that our peaceful relations would not last for long. I saw a challenge in his eye and went out to meet him halfway.

It was quite clear that Big Six was just looking for an opportunity and that he wouldn't be too particular about how one came about. It didn't take long. Someone asked a question about parliamentary procedure and Big Six insisted on holding on to the podium, to the exclusion of all others. He was an orator, completely used to this type of speech making, and could have given lessons to Daniel Webster himself. To hear him tell it, you would have thought he was the only person in Galveston qualified to discuss a point of law. I let him go on for about five minutes, then I decided it had gone on long enough. So I stood up and asked the president to bring us back to the matter at hand. The president did so, but Big Six refused to comply. He just looked at the president, laughing, and continued with his speech. He thought he would intimidate everyone by the power of his eloquence and in fact, I do remember that he made a real impression on most of the people in the room. But this little game could only go on for so long with Jack Johnson. I let him continue for as long as I could without losing my patience, and then I went over to him. When I was standing right next to him, I started yelling in his ear, several times louder than he: "Mr. President, didn't you order this gentleman to sit down?"

Big Six jumped, which is not surprising, since I had put my mouth right next to his ear and shouted at the top of my lungs. He was so stunned by my interruption that he stopped short, staring at me, his mouth hanging half open and his right arm lifted to heaven, which he had been invoking when I cut him off.

"Mr. President, have I heard you correctly or are my ears playing tricks on me?" I continued, not giving Big Six a second to clear his head.

The president had remained dumbfounded by my unexpected entrance into the ring, but summoned up enough courage to answer my question in a manner that was less than heroic: "Mr. Johnson, you must have heard me call the gentleman back to the matter at hand," he said in a hesitant voice.

"Very well then," I replied, lowering my voice. "If this gentleman who insists on talking when no one wants to listen to him and who refuses to sit down when he has received an order from the president to do so, cannot be silenced in any other way, I demand that we call a policeman to escort him out."

My words were met by a profound silence. Big Six was so nonplussed by my audacity that he was unable to say a word. I saw his lips move but the words didn't come out. Everyone in the room was anxious and wondering what was going to happen. Finally, my adversary made a grumbling sort of noise; putting his right hand on my shoulder, he said in a half whisper: "Come on, Jack, you and I have always been friends. Let's not start arguing."

His mild manner didn't fool me for a second. I could see in his eyes that he was plotting something, something that would do me no good. I don't know how it works, but when you look into a man's eyes, you can almost always almost tell when he's going to attack you or is getting ready to throw a punch at you. Through much experience, I can even guess what type of punch and defend myself accordingly. But this is not always accurate. Sometimes, you expect a roundhouse and an uppercut comes at you. In that case, you just have to be faster than the other guy and block it. I don't understand how this sort of mental transmission takes place; I use the advantage it gives me and leave the task of explaining it to people smarter than I.

In the case of Big Six, it worked like a charm. I realized that he was getting ready to pull something on me. Although he was stronger and heavier than

I was, I was sure he wouldn't attack me fairly. I expected him to pull out his revolver but I didn't give him time to do it. Before he could make a move, I landed a right hand on his jaw, putting all my strength and all my weight behind it. Big Six crumbled to the floor, taking two or three chairs down with him, and fell from the platform onto the ground.

His big body hadn't even touched the ground before half of the people in the room had already pulled out their revolvers and started shooting at random. I have never in my life seen so many shots fired without anyone being wounded. I have also never seen a room that big empty out that fast. Some were shoving their way out the door, others were jumping out the windows. In the blink of an eye, the only people left in the room were Big Six and me, but Big Six was still fast asleep.

Such were the beginnings of the political career I had in my neighborhood in Galveston. They did not lack, as you see, a certain animation. As for the candidacy in question, the committee hesitated and eventually the current president was kept on in his position. I didn't stay long in the milieu of politicians, whose struggles were too complicated and too tiring for me. I wasted no time getting back to the noble art, not to abandon it again.

Seven

JOE CHOYNSKI TEACHES ME WHAT
A KNOCKOUT IS

And so I resumed my career as a boxer, touring the country from St. Louis to Chicago to New York, and then back to Memphis, fighting everywhere I could manage to set up a match. I was on my way back to Galveston when I got held up for a week in Memphis by a flood of the Mississippi. I got to Galveston at the very same time as the famous and terrible flood of 1900, caused by a tidal wave. It was a dreadful catastrophe, the horrors of which I will never forget.

No member of my family died during that terrible period, but many of my friends lost their possessions or their lives in the disaster. For once, my strength and my endurance were useful. When our house collapsed beneath the raging flood, I managed to carry all the members of my family to safety. There wasn't a single family in our neighborhood that didn't have the loss of one or several members to grieve. I was lucky enough to put all the many Johnsons I cherished out of harm's way.

Once the danger had passed, my mother thanked the Lord that her Jack had been able to save her from the waves. I couldn't resist the temptation to remind her of the many times she had regretted the strength of my muscles, doing everything in her power to turn me away from the profession of boxer.

"You have to admit, Mama, that I am still good for something," I said to her, laughing. "Admit it!"

"It's true, son, you could whip the devil and all the hounds of hell."

That made me happier than all the thanks and all the rewards I could possibly receive in those troubled times. I worked like a demon for more than a week, steering boats and pushing rafts, to try to save the poor pieces of furniture and other debris that were floating here and there at the mercy of the waves. Everyone was doing as I was, but I didn't have any weakness in my chosen work as a salvager to be ashamed of. It was nonetheless a tough time and I wouldn't wish it on anyone.

After that, I had so many fights that I can't remember them all. I fought many men who were taller and heavier than I, but my career wasn't going the way I wanted it to. I hadn't yet managed to fight a great boxer and I had to do that if I wanted to make a name for myself in the profession.

Nonetheless, I was coming along more quickly than I was aware of. All the sportsmen in the region knew who Jack Johnson was and they were all talking about him. Some of them weren't saying good things. I am sure that they didn't understand me. It would be a long time after that before they did. They reproached me for many faults. I may have deserved some of their criticism, but they were wrong in much of their evaluation of me and of my skill as a boxer. I wasn't aggressive enough, according to them. I stayed on the defensive too much. It took me too long to make my move. I couldn't explain to them that what I was doing was learning how to box. For me, it was an ongoing lesson and I learned from all my opponents, big and small. When I was in the ring, my opponent was a teacher. I would study his every move, like you study the movements of a machine. Most of the men I fought had the advantage, which I didn't, of having had lessons from a scientific boxer. I had never had enough money to pay for a teacher. What little I knew I had learned from the tough and painful school of hard knocks.

If I had explained all that, people would probably have made fun of me and said that I was a typical yellow nigger. The folks who came to see me in the ring thought that I was there to hit, to do damage, and to take my opponent out. They would have said that they came to see me fight, not take a lesson. No one would have thought that this big, poor nigger was in the process of methodically learning his craft, with the firm intention of increasing, little by little and through a tough form of education, his knowledge of the sport of boxing. I followed the plan I had set out for myself, without worrying about criticism from people who preferred to think that I was an animal without intelligence, making his way as a fighter thanks only to his brute force. As for me, I thought that each bit of progress was a step in the right direction, the direction of a career that I pursued tirelessly.

At long last, I left my period of obscurity behind me. I was going to fight a genuine champion, Joe Choynski. Jack Johnson was the happiest nigger in the entire United States when it was decided that he would fight this man, who was universally famous. The moment had come when I was finally going to get a real boxing lesson. I was going to be looking across the ring at one of the best boxers in the world; all I would have to do is study him.

The lesson was brief but it was among those that I have never forgotten, and it has served me well. I can't say I was nervous when I got into the ring and looked across at the famous California heavyweight, but I must admit that I was a bit concerned. I had achieved the goal I had been seeking for a long time, my first fight with a champion; the success or failure of my entire life depended on the outcome. Naturally, I never thought for a second that I could beat Choynski. The best I could hope for was to stay in there with him for a few rounds. What I wanted above all was, when he did knock me out, to be able to figure out how he had done it.

No, I will never forget that fight, which took place before the members of the Galveston Athletic Club in March 1901. I was twenty-two years old and in excellent condition, but as bumbling in the ring as it is possible to be. Joe and I had never seen each other before the fight; he tried to find out from some of my friends in Galveston what sort of man he was going to have in front of him.

They told him that it was useless to try to wear me down, that I had the strength and stamina of a horse, and that his best plan would be to go after me quick and hard, before I had the chance to land a punch or two. This was excellent advice and Joe proved himself to be a clever man by following it.

From the minute he climbed into the ring and took his robe off, I never stopped studying him—that is, until I visited the land of dreams for a few seconds thanks to one of his scientific punches.

First of all, I made a quick study of his legs, his body, his shoulders, his arms, and his face. I saw that I had the advantage in weight, height, reach, and strength. But Choynski had something I lacked, and I was fully aware of it: skill. That was ten years ago and since then I've acquired some experience.

I acquitted myself pretty well in the first and second rounds and he must have thought I was an opponent not to be disdained. It was at the very beginning of the third round that something—it happened so fast that I didn't see it coming—landed on my jaw, with a precision that left no doubt as to its origin. I may not have known at the time what it was, but I have since learned that it was a "right hook." Since then, I myself have used this elegant means of persuasion fairly often, but that day, when it hit me, I was no longer interested, for a moment anyway, in the things of this world.

I met up with Choynski again at the defendants' table in a courtroom. Governor Sayers had little appreciation for the noble art and he decided to make an example of us. The days that followed were extremely unpleasant for us both, as they took place in isolation, two weeks' worth. It was only after this little vacation that we were released, like two thugs who had attacked some upstanding citizen on a street corner. A special session of the Texas State Legislature was called, to pass a law criminalizing boxing matches. But we each put down $500 bail and left the state before the law was promulgated.

Sheriff Henry Thomas was a delightful man. He gave Joe and me the royal treatment. He allowed the club to send us boxing gloves and every day we would box in the jail yard, surrounded by police officers and guests. Joe had great affection for me and to prove it, he gave me lessons, showing me the best punches anyone has ever seen in a jail yard. I learned more in those two weeks than I had learned in my entire existence up to that point. Besides, we didn't have anything to do other than sleep, eat, box, and talk; I saw to it that the boxing part was not neglected.

So those two weeks in jail were an extremely lucky thing for me. Unfortunately, our arrest bankrupted the club and I had to go elsewhere to exercise my profession. But from then on I had the precious help of Joe Choynski, who did everything he could to make me a champion.

For the next two years, because of the law passed by the Texas Legislature, which made it impossible for me to practice my profession in my home state, I had to travel all over the place, fighting any colored man who would accept my challenge.

I won all of those many fights, but they earned me only a modest reputation and even less in the way of money.

I hadn't forgotten the way Klondike had beaten me in the last five rounds of our match in Chicago the year before, so I left for Memphis to set up a rematch with the Black Adonis. The result of the fight proved to me that I had made great progress and, on the other hand, that Klondike was as good a fighter as ever. For twenty rounds, we showed each other no mercy and I was happy to hear the referee declare the match a draw.

"Next time, Mr. Johnson," my opponent said, "I really think you're going to beat me."

These were the words he spoke as he left the ring. I laughingly responded: "Give me the chance to make your prediction come true!"

Klondike promised he would and he kept his word. The following year, I fought him again and in the thirteenth round, I put him to sleep. That proved to me that the number thirteen brings me luck, regardless of what superstitious minds may claim.

Eight

I FIGHT FOR BEANS!

Between these various contests, I often went through unfortunate periods. Lack of money was an ongoing problem and I frequently arrived in a city without a red cent in my pocket.

"Little Artha," I would say to myself to give myself courage (the sportsmen had already given me the nickname at that point), "you just have to work things out."

I indeed had to use the most fantastic methods to procure a little money for myself while I waited to sign a contract for a fight. Sometimes, without a contract, I would go into bars, hoping to find some generous souls who would give me the few coins I needed to pay for a bed to sleep in.

And if I didn't meet up with any generous souls, I often spent the night outside. One day, I got to Pittsburgh without a penny to my name. I didn't even have enough to buy a plate of beans. I didn't like the city one bit, even less because there weren't any fights going on there. I waited impatiently to get back on the road East. Someone advised me to go to the slaughterhouses and try to sneak onto a freight train on its way out. I followed this advice and while I was walking through the yards of the slaughterhouses, a slaughter man, who knew what kind of financial state I was in, asked me if I knew how to box:

"I see what you're getting at!" I answered. "Are you telling me there's a way to make a little money around here?"

"Fact is, we have a very strong, very well built man who has knocked out every man who's stood up to him. Do you want to put on the gloves with him?"

Not being in a state of mind to waste any time, I simply asked:

"How much money are we talking?"

"However much we take in when we pass the hat around the crowd. I guarantee it'll be enough to buy beans for a few weeks."

"In that case, I'm your man! When will the festivities take place?"

"This very evening."

He wanted to give me a bit of advice:

"If you're bluffing," he said in a very serious tone, "and you're not a real fighter, don't fight this guy. He has been in the ring more than a few times and has knocked out a number of first-rate boxers!"

"Just bring him to me and I'll finish him off!"

"You must really be starving," he said.

If he had had any idea how starved I was, he would no doubt have invited me to lunch, but the idea didn't even cross his mind. The fight took place that same evening in the yard of the slaughterhouses. From the time I laid eyes on him, I realized that the man I was going to fight was pretty tough and that it wasn't going to be a walk in the park for me. I also saw that he wasn't afraid of me and that he figured it would be an easy win for him. One thing is sure: the fight was for real!

I wasn't in very good condition; it's hard to be in good shape when you haven't eaten for several days. Little by little, I went to work in earnest and I did the best I could. It took me twenty minutes of hard labor to convince that boxer that he had made a serious mistake by agreeing to fight me. By the time he gave up, I admit that I had taken some terrific punches. The crowd was enormously pleased with the battle, the benefits of which fell to me alone, by the way. When they gave me the proceeds of the passing of the hat, I realized that I had come into possession of a lump sum of $75, almost all of it in silver coins.

That was nine years ago . . . and I can still feel that seventy-five dollars in my hand! Oh my, that beautiful seventy-five dollars! Oh my, those delicious dollars! They meant more to me than a million dollars does to John D. Rockefeller. I wanted to go right out and buy a whole case of beans!

But there was something more important to Jack Johnson than beans. I wanted to travel in softly upholstered train compartments, not cattle-cars.

All these experiences served me well, though. And I cannot tell you how happy I am today that I had to defend myself against adversity and know poverty as intimately as I did. I've been around the world three times and around the United States many more times than that. Most of the time I had money but how many times did I not have a penny to my name! Now that I have managed to clear a path all the way to the world championship, all those experiences—many of which were terribly painful at the time—really seem very funny to me. I like to talk about them when I don't have anything better to do.

The saddest moments of my career as a fighter came about because of the so-called color question people are always going on about. I have noticed many times that a fighter of ordinary abilities doesn't make himself very popular by bringing up the line demarcating whites from blacks too much. That line caused me a lot of trouble in my early years. But now I'm used to it and don't even notice it any more.

It seems to me that boxers are not well qualified to comment on social questions: let them stick to their gloves and to the ring and not bother us with their preferences about color. It doesn't matter much to the public if a champion is black, white, green, or red. What they want is for him to be a good boxer, always courageous, and to fight as cleanly as possible. A true fighter should be able to, and want to, fight anyone with enough talent to aspire to the title. And that means not building a wall around himself, the gate of which is strictly forbidden to anyone likely to beat him. When Mr. Champion starts discussing questions of color, you can bet he has excellent reasons to do so.

Several years ago, some very good featherweights brought up this hatred of the black man so as to avoid having to fight marvelous little George Dixon. Perhaps there would have been fewer highly ranked featherweights if that animosity hadn't existed. Tommy Ryan's thoughts about the color question were without a doubt provoked by Joe Walcott and everyone in sporting circles today knows it. Knowing Joe as I did when he was at the top of his form, I am not surprised that Tommy used any excuse he could get hold of, as long as it served to keep him away from Walcott. Even poor old John L. Sullivan, one of the most upstanding fighters the world has ever known, dressed himself up in that prejudice called "the color line." Peter Jackson was at the top of his form at that point, as you know. And I will bet dollars to doughnuts that Jimmy Britt's preference for that imaginary color line was inspired by the idea of Joe Gans. Do you remember, for example, Gentleman J. Britt, how you forgot all your scruples about color the day you were sure, really sure, that you could beat Joe?[1]

Now that I have definitively settled the color question, I can speak to you more at my leisure and go back to my memoirs where I left them.

What I said about that matter will nonetheless serve to explain how it is that almost all my fights were against men of color. Black men have so much trouble finding white opponents that everyone was amazed that Joe Choynski agreed to get in the ring with me in Galveston. Lots of people thought he figured he was setting himself an easy task. The truth of the matter is quite different: he simply wasn't used to judging a man by his color.

In 1902, I took part in fifteen fights. I won eleven of them and got a draw in four. The five men I knocked out that year were: Dan Murphy, in the tenth round; Ed Johnson, in the fourth; Jack Jeffries, the enormous brother of the former world champion whom I went on to beat later. Jack, who was an excellent boxer, got put out of commission in the fifth round. Finally, I put my old pal Klondike to sleep in the thirteenth.[2] The men I fought to a draw were: Frank Childs (six rounds), Billy Stift (ten rounds), and Hank Griffin twice, in the twentieth and fifteenth rounds respectively.

In all those fights, I never once tried to win by knockout. I was studying boxing. I wanted to learn as much as I could and beat my opponents on points. I don't like to brag, but I could have knocked out my opponents and gotten things over with a whole lot quicker, if my great desire hadn't been to use those matches as a form of training.

In the four draws, I could have knocked out any one of my rivals in two or three rounds. But in my last contest with Hank Griffin, I was delighted to get the draw, because at that time, Hank was truly a hard man to beat.

In early 1903, I was in California. I had been lucky enough to acquire a number of friends on the West Coast. A lot of them were eager to know what I could do in the ring. As you might well guess, I was as eager as they were to show what I had learned in the school of hard knocks, where I had been taking classes for several years. Furthermore, I knew that my reputation as a "coward" had traveled across the country and I wanted more than anything to issue the most categorical proof to the contrary of this assertion.

It was not very hard for the promoters to convince me to sign on for a match with Denver Ed Martin, in spite of the fact that the purse was not the most enticing I had seen. After a number of wasted days, due to difficulties provoked by Martin's camp, it was decided that the affair would take place on February 3, in Los Angeles. Ed had a splendid record and I knew that this match was worth traveling for, be it one or many miles. Based on everything I had heard about my rival, I knew he was different from all the other men I had fought up to that point. He had the reputation of fighting like a tornado. I concluded that I was at last going to have the chance, so long awaited, to put my skill to work.

I was not mistaken. In the very first minute, I realized that I was across the ring from one of the finest specimens of the colored race who ever set foot inside a boxing ring. He was five years older than I. We weighed nearly the same and were nearly the same height. This was a pugilist who had a lot of fans present at every one of his fights. He had been marvelously well trained, with the goal of putting an end to my pretensions of winning a championship of any kind. I saw in his eyes all the resolute will he had mustered in order to beat me. And yet he was smiling. He shook my hand with great cordiality, as if we were being introduced in someone's parlor. Despite his affectionate countenance, I remembered the right hook Joe Choynski had landed on me in the first important match of my career. That bitter memory didn't fail to bring me back to the reality of the situation at hand. This time I wasn't going to fall victim to the same kind of punch.

"I do regret having to knock down such a cute and charming little thing as yourself," he laughed, with a disdainful but affable look on his face.

"Don't you worry about that," I answered. "When I'm finished with you, my little friend, you might well be a whole lot prettier than you are right now. For your sake, I certainly hope so!"

The first round looked more like a waltz than a boxing bout. The two of us circled around the ring on tiptoes more than six or seven times without daring to get near each other. We were each trying to get the other to attack. Finally, Ed lunged at me and managed to give me a nice little love tap on the nose, the result of which was a nice little nosebleed.

"Many thanks," I called out to him from my corner during the break between rounds. "I have so much blood in my veins that I always have my doctor bleed me before I get into the ring. As it happens, I forgot to do it today and I am infinitely grateful to you for taking care of it for me."

The crowd doubled over laughing at that response. Ed himself couldn't help being won over by the general hilarity.

In the second round, we kept on dancing the two-step. I must admit that the audience didn't seem to take much interest in our twirling around and around. From every corner of the room, these words rang out:

"Enough with the cake-walk! Enough with the cake-walk!"

At that very moment, Ed rushed at me like a whirlwind and landed a terrific hook to my left cheek, a punch so hard it broke his metacarpal. In any case, my cheek remembered that shock for a long time to come.

The ease with which he had landed a punch on me gave my opponent an excess of confidence and I answered with a sledgehammer blow that sent three of his teeth flying out onto the padded canvas of the ring. I was truly sorry for him: they were so delightfully pretty, with their gold caps! I can assure you they added nothing to his beauty, luckily for him. Like me, the spectators found the incident extremely funny.

It wasn't until the twelfth round that we got to work for real. Until then, we had both thrown only occasional punches.

The fight had been even. Although we were both bleeding in various places, neither one of us seemed to have had enough. On the contrary. Nonetheless it seemed to me—and I perceived this with genuine pleasure—that Denver was unable to hit me with enough force to end the fight. Consequently, I was able to gain confidence and trust in my usual tactic, winning on points. I took real pleasure in this little game and the crowd got to see a beautiful fight.

I saw no reason whatsoever compelling me to finish things before the scheduled number of rounds. By the seventeenth round, Ed was so out of breath he sounded like a seal. He was bleeding so much that during the rest periods several men would go to work wiping streams of it off his body. I put to work all the skill I had trying to do everything just right. From the thirteenth to the twentieth round, I prevented my opponent from landing a single punch. At the end of the fight, I was awarded the decision on points. The spectators cheered and applauded, proving their satisfaction and even their enthusiasm. Ed and I parted as good friends.

"You are certainly the better man of the two of us, Mistah Johnson," Denver Martin confessed to me, "and I consider it a great honor to have fought you."

From that day on, my reputation as a chicken had come to an end. I had proved that I intended to stick with my chosen profession as a boxer, and that I was as eager to be a decent, upstanding fighter as any man, white or black.

All the people who had placed their faith in me were delighted by my victory and made me promise to continue my ascension toward the upper echelons of the sport.

Nine

MY OLD FRIEND SAM McVEY

A few weeks later, I signed a contract to fight Sam McVey, the great colored boxer, who later became the idol of the French public for several years.

The fight was supposed to take place in the same ring in which I had already won my victory over Ed Martin. The date was set for three weeks later. I had no time to rest. The very day after my fight with Martin, I started training again, which meant above all, eating three square meals a day, quite a switch from the days when I looked on with envy as some poor rascal made a feast of a plate of beans in the streets of Boston. I was certainly doing enough exercise to give me a ferocious appetite. I didn't have to worry in those days about getting too fat. I knew perfectly well that Sam McVey was a tough man to beat. I had seen him sparring at the club a number of times and realized that he knew more about boxing than any other pugilist I had fought, with the exception of Joe Choynski. He was heavier than me and very quick on his feet.

In spite of all that, before the tenth round of our match on February 27, 1903, I felt sure that I had won the decision on points and didn't need to put myself to any more trouble. We continued fighting through the twentieth round and I did in fact win the decision.

After the fight, several critics went so far as to say that the two of us had been equal and that only chance could have made the scales tip in favor of one or the other. This remark gave me a good laugh: I knew perfectly well that it would have been very easy for me to finish the fight after the twelfth round if I had wanted to. I preferred to finish the match with skill and that's what I did.

This opinion put forth by certain journalists encouraged Sam and his partisans. From the minute they heard it, they were eager to sign for a rematch with me. And that's what happened, almost immediately. I waited only for the necessary funds to be raised to offer me a sufficiently large purse. The fight was held on October 27 and the outcome was identical. In fact, the second fight was so similar to the first one that I will spare you an account of it.

Nonetheless, Sam McVey and his friends were not satisfied. My opponent was as convinced he could beat me as I was of the contrary. He hounded me until I gave him yet another chance to beat me. We fought in San Francisco, on April 22 of the following year, in a match in which I knocked him out in the twentieth round.

It was only at that point that all the sportsmen, including Sam himself, realized that he was not in the same league with me. After my second fight in Los Angeles, the California promoters wanted to put me back to work so badly that they looked high and low to find a man able to put up a decent fight against me. Their efforts were in vain. No one seemed to want to meet up with me in the ring, and I had to travel back across the continent in order to get some work. Now that I was well established in my profession, I didn't want to get rusty; so I left for Boston, where the sportsmen did their best to find someone willing to fight me.

At that time, people in sporting circles were talking a lot about Sandy Ferguson. Some of the know-it-alls thought he was an up-and-comer, the sure-fire successor to Jim Jeffries' title as champion. At first, Ferguson didn't seem entirely committed to signing on for a match with me. I suppose the stupid question of color played a big part in his incomprehensible hesitation. Maybe it was also because some candid friends had told him how well they thought of me and described what I had accomplished on the West Coast. But finally the match was set up.

When we met up in the ring, I realized that I was dealing with a powerful man, for sure, but one better suited to wrestling than boxing. So making him look like a rank amateur was an easy task for me, as was winning the bout in ten rounds.

I then went to Philadelphia to satisfy the curiosity of Joe Butler, a colored pugilist, who thought it would be the easiest thing in the world to make me disappear from the pugilistic horizon. Three rounds sufficed to demonstrate to Joseph that he had made the grossest of errors.

Sandy Ferguson made an appearance in the Quaker City and tried to spread the rumor that I had hypnotized him during our fight in Boston. To this he added, without the slightest modesty that he was the real up-and-comer, the future champion, and the best boxer in the world, next to whom Jeffries would look like a wretched little amateur.

So we fought a six-round no-decision match. To tell the truth, I have never really understood the hypocritical no-decision matches that some American cities require. Those municipalities certainly have no more than a distant relation to the sport of boxing.

I cannot bring myself to understand how there could have been no decision in my second fight with Sandy Ferguson, in Philadelphia. A few of my friends were inclined to undertake an investigation of the matter, but I really didn't have time to lose for such a trifle.

Everyone who saw the six rounds of the bout acknowledged that the famous up-and-comer would have been utterly incapable of lasting one more round. He claimed afterward that both of his hands were already sprained when he got into the ring; he certainly fought as if that were the case. I don't really like to speak ill of my opponents, but the fact is that the people who had presented Sandy as the future wearer of the championship belt had very clearly put their feet in their mouths.

To make a long story short, Sandy followed me to California and, after my fight with Sam McVey, I agreed to give him a chance to rehabilitate himself. We found ourselves in each other's company once more on December 11, 1903, in Colma.

This fight was a replica of our previous match in Boston, in July of that same year. I let Sandy hang on until the twentieth round, because the spectators were so amused by our bout and I didn't have the heart to take that pleasure away from them. At the end of the twentieth round, a decision on points was handed down in my favor, and it was clear that Sandy was not really a worthy opponent for me. He was without a doubt the boxer to whom I did the most harm in a match and it still pains me to think about the pitiful state he was in when his seconds carried him out of the ring.

Ferguson was one of the rare men with whom my fights seemed less like boxing matches and more like personal grudges. I don't know if his animosity toward me was motivated by the wretched question of color. I assume the more likely problem was that he didn't appreciate the less-than-kind way I engaged him in conversation in the ring. In any case, he always looked at me like he was going to devour me. He proved himself so fearless in his attempts to do me physical harm that it was all his seconds could do to impress upon him the danger of being disqualified for a foul. This is in fact what happened in our last fight, in Chelsea (Mass.), on July 18, 1905. The future champion went after me with such fury that by the sixth round, he had completely forgotten that a sportsman by the name of the Marquess of Queensberry had ever existed. The result was my being declared the winner on a foul in the seventh round.

Ten

TWO FORMIDABLE OPPONENTS:
MARVIN HART AND SAM LANGFORD

1904 was a very peaceful year for me, the calmest I had spent since I started cultivating the noble art. As usual, all my opponents were colored men. A boxer who fought under the name of Black Bill was putting on some nice little exhibitions on the West Coast and a few of my Philadelphia friends urged me to go see if the man was a real champion. Although I thought I had given sufficient proof of my abilities, I didn't want to let my friends down and I consented to do what they wanted. This weakness on my part led to a bout that was so violent that the police intervened in the sixth round and there was no decision. Naturally, that was exactly what Black Bill's entourage wanted, because it gave him the chance to fight me a second time.

When my second fight with Black Bill took place, on May 3 of the following year, I was sure that it wouldn't be a repetition of the no-decision match, because I had decided that I would finish it in the fourth round.

Nonetheless, Black Bill and his friends still weren't satisfied and we fought again on July 13 of the same year, in Philadelphia. I, of course, had the advantage but things were finagled so that there was a non-decision in the sixth round. It wasn't until April 19, 1906, that I put an end, once and for all, to the pugilistic aspirations of this ring artist, by knocking him out in Wilkes-Barre, Pa.

In 1904, only four fights were set up for me. In two of them, I knocked out two of my old opponents: Sam McVey, in twenty rounds in San Francisco and Denver Ed Martin, in two rounds in Los Angeles. The two other fights that year were a no-decision match with Black Bill and another with my old friend Frank Childs. I beat the latter in six rounds, although I would have liked to make it last the full twenty. But one's predictions are sometimes wrong.

This reminds me of what I have always considered one of the most unpleasant memories of my career as a boxer. I am talking about my match with Marvin Hart on March 28, 1905, in San Francisco. Ever since the severe thrashing I received at the hands of Joe Choynski, in my own hometown of Galveston in 1901, I had put away all opponents, both large and small. I had begun to think that I could hold my own against any man with no more than two legs. The time had come for me to back off a little from the exaggerated opinion of Jack Johnson that I had developed.

I didn't know my future opponent personally, but based on everything we knew about his performances and how sure I was that we would be worthy of each other, I was overjoyed at the idea of finally fighting a man in my league. I delighted in advance in what I thought would be one of the best moments of my life.

I must say up front that the man in no way disappointed me; from the opening bell of the fight, his performance never failed for a moment to be interesting for all concerned. I nonetheless never doubted for a second that I could bring him down. I knew that I was completely dominating him and so did everyone in the crowd. I was so sure of my victory on points that I didn't think for an instant that I wouldn't get it. Imagine my surprise and disgust when the judge, at the end of the twentieth round, gave the win to Marvin Hart.

At least I had the satisfaction of seeing that the judge's decision did not meet with the approval of one single spectator, other than Hart and his personal friends. The event ended in an uproar; for a few minutes, it turned into an actual brawl. I didn't hesitate to declare that I had been robbed and the vast majority of the crowd agreed with me. It was plain as day that bets had been placed: the bettors had made arrangements with the judge and I was their victim. This is of course the sort of misadventure that takes place in the life of any boxer, but it was the first time I had experienced such a thing. I was so outraged that I swore never to fight again on the West Coast until the system in place had been changed. I packed my trunks and left the West the very day after the fight.

I arrived in Philadelphia with a very light wallet, but I found a number of deals, all of them advantageous, waiting for me. In the few months following my arrival, I had no fewer than seven bouts in the Quaker City, knocking out in succession Jim Jeffords, Walter Johnson, and Morris Harris. One of the men I fought at that time was Jack Munroe, from Butte, Montana, a miner who had held his own for four rounds against Jeffries.[1] In July of that year, I fought four times, squaring off against Morris Harris and Black Bill on the same day, July 15. In all, I had thirteen bouts that year. The last one took place on December 2, against Joe Jeannette, in Philadelphia, six rounds with no decision.

In 1906, I fought Joe Jeannette four times. Joe and I met up so often that it became a game for us and we genuinely enjoyed it. In our second fight, a six-rounder, a very serious match with lots of skill on both our parts, I lost on a foul in the second round. Later on that season, we fought again in Baltimore, and I won in fifteen rounds. I must admit that Joe Jeannette fought one of the most terrific fights of his life on that occasion.

In April 1906, Sam Langford and I met up for fifteen rounds in Chelsea, Mass., and I found him to be one of the toughest opponents I had ever faced in the ring. I weighed 190 pounds at that time and Langford only 138. In the second round, the little nigger landed a terrific right hand on my jaw and I went down like I had been hit by a cannonball. Never in my entire pugilistic career, neither before nor since, have I taken a punch that landed with that much force. It was all I could do to get back on my feet by the time the referee was about to count "Ten!" I managed to do that but I can assure you that I felt the effects of that punch for the rest of the fight. I realized at that moment that against a man like Langford, you can never let your guard down and that I needed to use all the skill I had. After fifteen rounds, I was declared the winner on points.

In May of that same year, I went to Gloucester, Mass., and sent Charlie Haghey off to Dreamland with just a few punches. Just one round was enough for me to demonstrate to him and his friends that he would do well to choose another profession. Then I returned to Philadelphia, where I fought a six-rounder, no decision, with Joe Jeannette. Jeannette was definitely my favorite partner. We put on another beautiful fight for the good people of Portland, Maine; those ten rounds ended in a draw.

Eleven

I MAKE SOME NEW YEAR'S RESOLUTIONS

Around that time, I started getting a little tired of the noble art of boxing, such as I practiced it. I was twenty-nine years old and had already had more bouts than any other boxer in the world, dead or alive. I had earned little money relative to the enormous amount of work I had done and I had put very little of it aside, virtually none. Furthermore, the future did not look terribly bright. If I had been older or wiser, things probably would have been different. But I was in the prime of youth and it felt good to be alive, even if I wasn't able to satisfy all my ambitions.

On the first day of January 1907, I sat myself down and resolved not to get back up until I had developed in my mind a clear idea of the current state of Jack Johnson. First of all, I tried to see myself as others saw me and not according to my own personal point of view. I took out a scrapbook in which I had pasted all the newspaper clippings about myself and looked for a description that seemed accurate. After lots of page turning, I finally came upon the following, which struck me as being as close to the truth as a newspaper article can get:

Johnson is as black as your hat. When he is in a good mood, which is most of the time, his big round face is completely lit up by his happy smile. His teeth are perfect and he knows it. Consequently he never misses a chance to show them to their best advantage. When he is out for a stroll, he looks like a real dandy and all his colored brothers are proud of him. He generally wears a big, flat white hat, checkered clothes, a gaudy vest, a colored shirt, gray or green spats, patent-leather shoes with very pointed toes and an enormous diamond as a tie-pin. His cane, as big around as a sapling, never leaves his side and his knotty fingers are covered with sparkling rings. He doesn't have much money, but he spends everything he's got on clothes and good meals. He smokes only black cigars and drinks only high-class spirits, when he can afford them. But his primary expense consists of the betterment of his physical condition. He is six feet tall, hard as a rock, and weighs 200 pounds stripped down. His arms are unbelievably long, like a gorilla's, and his black muscles look like a bundle of strands of wire.[1]

This description, as humorous as it is, was not in fact very far from the truth. Of course, the comparison to a gorilla wasn't exactly to my taste, but truth be told I had to admit that it wasn't entirely inaccurate. I came to the conclusion that if this was the opinion the public had of me, I had no grounds for complaint.

Then I started thinking about serious matters. I dug down deep into my mind and reflected on what life had in store for me. It was New Year's Day, remember, and the season for such reflection. Here's what I said to myself:

First of all, boxing should be a business for me. I am in this profession to get as much out of it as I can and my personal likes and dislikes have nothing to do with it, no more so than if I owned some sort of business. So I need a plan for making my fortune. Of course I am happy to have built up a record like mine at my age, but that was due to my natural abilities and I would be wrong to give myself too much glory for it. I admit that there was little merit in taking down some of the men I fought, but when I get it in my head to fight an opponent, neither his size nor his skill ever stops me. To be sure, I'm fool enough to rush at a man and try to put him to sleep with the first punch, on the pretext of finishing things in a single round. I generally believe that it is wiser to drag things out. I consider that much of my success as a boxer resides in the fact that I always have a very accurate idea of what my opponent can do and, simultaneously, a plan well thought out in advance for my own actions. I have rarely faced a man across the ring without predicting how he was going to conduct himself. One of the rare mistakes I remember having made was during my match with Sam Langford, when I let him land a punch on my jaw that very nearly sent me off to Dreamland.

The man who can knock me down at will has yet to be born. What happened to those prognosticators who thought I was a little chicken next to their great champions? Ask any of the men who have fought me how easy it is to put me on the canvas. The truth is, Jack, you haven't been stretched out for a full ten seconds since you were a novice. And yet you've never had to give your all. Each time you've won, you've always held a little something back, so that no one has ever taken your true measure. If people did see what I can do, there would be some mighty surprised faces around the ring! They would open their eyes good and wide if they ever saw me play the game all-out!

Such were the reflections in which I indulged on that first day of January 1907 and they made me happy. I realized that I wasn't ready to pack it in and that my pluses far outweighed my minuses. I was in an enviable position in the world and I swore to myself to stay there.

Abandon the ring? Never! I had already had fifty-five regular matches, not counting all the ones I had forgotten, and I was only twenty-nine years old.

You can see that I had an excellent opinion of myself, better perhaps than others had of me. That is completely natural, since I was the only person who knew why I had never become a knockout champion. The reasons why I had never let people see what I could do have been given so many times in these memoirs that I don't need to go over them again.

So I decided to continue in my career as a boxer and to try to rise above the terrible color question, if such a thing exists. For the twelve years and more that I had been in the ring, I had developed amazingly in terms of speed, skill, and fighting experience and had greatly increased my power. I had no intention of giving up my old methods. I wasn't an apprentice any more but I didn't want to get rusty either. I considered myself to be the equal of the best men out there and I'm not sure that, down deep, I didn't even consider myself a little better.

After all this thinking, which is no doubt less interesting for the reader to read than it was for me to do, I amused myself by searching my scrapbook for a different opinion. The person who wrote it must never have seen me anywhere but in the comic strips:

Handsome clothes, lots of them: enough diamonds to light up his shirtfront and his hands when he strolls through the streets, such are the primary ambitions of the distinguished gentleman known by the name of John Arthur Johnson. He aspires to replace the great Brummel and has pretensions of doing so whenever he appears in public. His great frame provides a completely suitable resting place for his latest-fashion suits and he can't but attract attention when he passes by in the street. He adores jewelry but prefers handsome clothes and would sacrifice anything to assure the smartness of his outfit. A few suits are not enough for him; he has to have at least twenty at a time. He changes clothes three or four times a day and his greatest joy would be to show off his entire wardrobe to the public.

Whenever he arrives in a city, his first concern is to unpack his trunks and hang up his clothes, which he handles with the greatest care. They never have the slightest mark on them and his pants always have the proper crease.

I wish you could have seen my mother's face when I read that clipping to her! When I got to the part where it talks about hanging my clothes, she lifted her hands to the sky and cried: "Oh no, child, I don't think you've ever hung anyone in your life!"

Twelve

I GO TO AUSTRALIA

It was around that same time that Alec McLean, who had been trying for several years to popularize boxing in Boston, started to get fed up with the difficulties he was encountering and invited me to take off with him for Australia. He told me that things couldn't be worse than in America and there was a good chance they would be better. I had been wanting to make that trip for a long time already, so McLean didn't need to insist. I looked forward to it with pleasure.

So we went to San Francisco and boarded ship. I hadn't forgotten my first, painful experience with salt water, but I certainly hoped not to renew it this time, now that I was a grown man in perfect condition instead of the exhausted, malnourished little kid I was before. Never in my life had I been so grossly mistaken. We hadn't yet lost sight of land when I started feeling weak. I stood up to go down to my cabin, but before I could take a step, I realized that my legs didn't want to carry me. They refused to render any service whatsoever and I sat down on the steps, my arms hanging onto the copper banisters.

Good God, I felt funny! It wasn't at all like the sickness I had experienced on my first trip. My stomach didn't feel good at all and I felt like I was drunk, dazed, and as weak as a child. I couldn't have gotten to my cabin on my own if a $100,000 purse had been waiting for me there. It was literally impossible for me to move.

Eventually, two stewards arrived. One got on each side of me and they tried to lift me up and set me on my feet. But I wouldn't have stayed upright for a single second if they hadn't been bolstering me.

I was completely alert but had lost all control over my body and finally the two men just had to carry me. They placed me on the couch, fully clothed. Then one of them took off my high-button shoes and my socks and slipped some pajamas on me (I have no idea how he did it, as I certainly wasn't helping him in any way).

I stayed like that for three days, as completely knocked out as I had been by Joe Choynski, the only man ever to send me to Dreamland. I was perfectly aware of what was going on around me, but was unable to do so much as lift my little finger. I should tell you straight away that the footman assigned to my room knew what was going on during those three days. He was truly lucky that I was unable to get my hands on him, because if I had been able to move, he would have had a might bad time of it for a quarter-hour or so. Every time he stuck his head in the cabin and asked, "So, sir, how are you feeling now?" I can't explain it but there was something in the man's voice that exasperated me. I could have killed him.

The worst was when he would ask me if I wanted to eat something and proceed to enumerate all the specials of the day.

"Does sir not want a slice of roast beef?" he would say with a smile that enraged me. "With potatoes? Or perhaps a slice of ham?"

And he would run away as if he was afraid I was going to be able to catch him. The third day, Alec McLean decided to leave the smoking room and stick his head in my cabin.

"How do you feel, Jack?" he asked. If he had been a sensitive man, he would hardly have appreciated my response. But he just laughed and returned to his poker and brandy and soda.

The morning of the fourth day, I started to feel a little bit like myself again. I still couldn't allow myself to even think of eating anything, but I did manage to sit up and take stock of what was going on. I wondered if I would ever be able to get back on my feet again but didn't venture to do so. Around noon, the steward arrived with a big bunch of purple grapes in his hand. The grapes reminded me of my old mother, because I always bought grapes (just like the ones I had just been brought) for her when she was sick.

I remembered what she would always say and that memory was the first pleasant sensation I had had in four days.

"Praise the Lord, child! This bunch of grapes is like the one the Bible tells us Moses' spies brought back from the land of Canaan. Twelve men could barely carry it on their shoulders!"

The steward didn't say a word, but he hung the bunch above my head, beside my bunk. He smiled and left me alone with the fruit. They were truly superb grapes, but at first I had no desire for them. It seemed like the effort to grab them and pick a grape from the bunch would be too much. After about an hour, I decided to put a little cluster in my mouth. Lord above! Never in my life had I tasted anything so good.

As I was finishing the last morsel and wondering if there were any more, the waiter came back:

"Ah! Ah!" he said. "I see you're feeling better, sir. Would you like something to eat?"

"I certainly would," I answered, in a voice that even I didn't recognize. "Bring me another bunch of grapes."

The man laughed and shook his head.

"You strike me as a discerning gourmet," he said. "But you shouldn't kid yourself that there are grapes growing on this boat. Every one of those bunches costs at least five shillings. I took the one I brought you off the captain's table."

"I couldn't care less where you got it, my boy," I replied. "But if you don't bring me another one, and on the double, your life won't be worth a plug nickel."

"Ah! Very well then," he said as he ran away. "If you're going to be like that, I'll see what I can do for you."

A few minutes later, he brought me a plateful of grapes. The freshness of that fruit did me a world of good and I tried to drink a cup of "beef tea." Then I worked up to something more substantial and less than a day later, I was consuming everything on the menu, without exception, not to mention a few "welsh rarebits" and other substantial supplementary snacks.

One of the first things I said to Alec McLean was that he should be prepared to go back to America without me, because if I ever managed to get on dry land again, no one would ever get me to leave it again in this life. Alec laughed and told me that he wasn't going to lose any sleep over it.

"Come on, pal," he said. "You won't be in Australia a week before you'll be asking to go back to America."

"Is it that bad? Then why did you get me mixed up in this business?"

"Oh, I'm hoping we're going to make a buck or two, if you ever get back in shape."

"Don't you worry about that. All I have to do is keep up this wonderful appetite for a few more days and I'll be the strongest man they've ever seen in this country."

Soon we were approaching Sydney. I forgot all my ills and was truly sorry to leave the charming friends I had made during the crossing. For the first time in my life, I experienced the pleasure of being in the company of people who didn't take other people's color into account. One of the most pleasant acquaintances I made on the boat was that of a rich planter, a Scotsman who invited me to spend ten days with him on his plantation. He promised to take me on hunts the likes of which we didn't have in America. I promised to take him up on his invitation, if I could arrange my affairs so as to make it possible.

The most amusing thing about all of this was that my Scottish friend, Mr. Malcolm Geddes, took a dislike to Alec McLean. One evening when we were strolling on deck, he told me that he didn't like to see me in such low company. He said that Alec was an unredeemably vulgar sort and not a worthy associate for me.

"I would prefer to have you come visit me by yourself," he added, "but if you prefer, I will also invite your American friend, even though I don't like him one bit."

When I told this to Alec, he nearly fell on the floor laughing. I didn't see what he found so funny about it, but he didn't seem offended in the slightest degree. He advised me to accept the invitation and added that he did not insist on accompanying me, under the circumstances, although, deep down, he would have really liked to.

Thirteen

I GO KANGAROO HUNTING

After I had been in the country for a few days I went to Mr. Geddes' farm, where I was treated like royalty. Alec didn't come with me. Many times I wished he were there, if only so that I could show him how well I was being received. Nothing was too good for me. My host enjoyed letting everyone know that they should give me any and everything that might please me. The farm, or "station" as they say down there, was one of the biggest in New South Wales, almost as big as many counties in America. The largest part consisted of thickets, where families of kangaroos, cassowaries, and other animals you often see in menageries, but nowhere else, lived. Mr. Geddes was a breeder of livestock and he told me he owned about 80,000 head. The exact number was impossible to calculate.

This took place in February, which is high summer in Australia. The grounds were covered with abundant lawns and everything was deliciously fresh. It had rained prodigiously in the days preceding my arrival and the streams were nearly overflowing their banks. It was an excellent season for farm work, but it was equally propitious for hunting.

Mr. Geddes employed about fifty workers in his house and owned more than 200 horses. As soon as I arrived, two good saddle horses were loaned to me, both of them trained for kangaroo hunting. My youthful experiences in America, as a stable boy, jockey, and horse trainer in Galveston, had made an excellent horseman of me. I couldn't wait to meet up with some kangaroos, who are, it seems, excellent boxers!

The day after my arrival, I was up with the sun, meaning at 4 A.M. We took enough provisions to last four days and a half-dozen blankets, in case we had to spend the night under the stars. In that delicious climate, no other protection was necessary. It was hot and dry, but it's ordinarily not that hot in Australia. We brought along eight dogs, all of them well trained for the sport, and were armed with Winchester repeating rifles.

We couldn't move very fast because the horses were laden down with provisions. So it was noon before we arrived on the banks of the little river where we had decided to set up camp. You can be sure that our little eight-hour-long amble had left us with mighty empty stomachs! The horses on which we had put our baggage were unsaddled and they started eating with a hunger that equaled our own. One of the men lit a big fire and started boiling water. Although I was the only coffee-drinker among the hunters, they were kind enough to make me a big pot, with excellent condensed milk to go with it. Mr. Geddes and two other members of the expedition drank tea without milk, because milk was very scarce on the farm and what little they had set aside for his two children. We ate ample portions of cold roast beef with rye bread and a cake I will remember for years to come.

During the entire expedition, we saw troops of kangaroos and it was all we could do to keep the dogs from chasing after them. If we had let them, the dogs would have been worn out before we even got to the designated spot. When we got there, some of them already had hurt paws and seemed very tired. I have never seen as much prey anywhere as kangaroos during that excursion. There were thousands of them and I will not reduce that estimate by a single head, as I am certain that it is an understatement. They came in all sizes, from little ones up to the seven-foot-tall ones they call "old men." Between the two extremes, you saw all the possible and imaginable varieties of kangaroos.

They are all gifted with extraordinary speed. You can't say that they run, in the strictest sense of the term, but I can assure you they cover ground faster than a Southern Pacific train. And I can also promise you that their speed is multiplied tenfold when there's a man or a dog at their heels. Mr. Geddes swore to me that he had seen kangaroos stride more than seven or eight yards at a time. Don't you think that's carrying things a bit too far?

But let's get back to the story of our hunt. Six of us and five dogs followed along the banks of the river. I had a good Winchester rifle with me. I was lucky from the very first shot and, thanks to Mr. Geddes' excellent lessons, I shot a superb "old man" who was lolling around, forty meters or so away. A few seconds later, we found ourselves in the middle of a troop. Since it wasn't interesting just to kill them with rifles, we decided to go help the dogs.

Those Australian dogs are marvelously well trained for kangaroo hunting; it was a revelation for me to see how they went about it. They would leap on the animal at the very moment he was starting to jump, which always made him fall backwards, thereby breaking his neck or becoming so dizzy that it was easy for the dog to grab hold of him. I pointed out to Mr. Geddes that it was a shame that the kangaroos put up so little fight, adding that it was hard to call something so easy a sport. My friend responded that some of the "old men" were a match for any dog. Some of them are cunning enough to know that their only means of defense consists of leaning up against a tree and keeping the dogs at bay. If the dog gets too close to the kangaroo, the kangaroo grabs him with his forearm and squeezes him as hard as he can, all the while hitting him with his back paw, which has terrible claws on it. Mr. Geddes added that a dog that has ever been grabbed like that by a kangaroo, even once, would never again attempt to attack one dead-on. Usually, he will just circle around the animal and bark until the other dogs came to his rescue.

On the other side of the river, the land was completely open and we saw kangaroos swarming in all directions. I thought it was completely unsportsmanlike to slaughter the poor beasts while they were being hounded by the dogs, so I told my host that I was going to try to chase one down instead.

I had a very lively mare and thought that a race through the countryside would really be very pleasant. I dug my spurs into my mare's belly and she took off at top speed. For three-quarters of a mile, we ran like the wind across the plain. My mare seemed to enjoy the chase and give it her all. Eventually, I got so close to the animal I was hunting that I was able to hit it with the knob of my riding crop, at which point he fell on the ground.

After that, there was a heart-stopping race between our best dogs and a very fast kangaroo. The kangaroo headed off toward a very dense thicket about a quarter of a mile away; if he managed to get there, he would certainly get away from us. The poor animal knew full well that his only chance of salvation was to get to that thicket, so he was moving as fast as lightning. He was going to make it, when he found himself in front of a puddle of water. Instead of leaping over it, the terrified animal jumped into it and sank down into the mud. Already our dogs had him surrounded and were barking terribly. I told Mr. Geddes that the poor beast surely deserved to live for having defended himself so well; at my request, the Scotsman agreed to spare him. I thus had one less kangaroo on my conscience.

Truth be told, that first and only kangaroo hunt was enough for me. It's not a sport for an American. Personally, I would rather find myself facing cougars or wild boars, like Jeffries did in Colorado. At least that's what he says. But he was the only one, besides an Indian chief, on that hunting party. And, ever since Captain Cook's Eskimos, we all know how much store to set by the testimony of an Indian. When I went out there to hunt, I heard an entirely different version of the story.

I spent several more very pleasant days on the farm. Mr. and Mrs. Geddes were charming to me and treated me as if I were some illustrious personage.

When I returned to Sydney, I had no cause to be anything but delighted with the business arrangements McLean had made. For his part, he didn't seem at all jealous of my newfound friendships, although he was himself of Scottish heritage. Before I left, I had invited my hosts to come to Sydney to attend my fight with Peter Felix. The match had been arranged before I went to the farm and Alec and I had thought that my stay out there would provide an excellent form of training. But Mr. Geddes just shook his head and told me he didn't approve at all of prizefights. His last words to me, as he left me at the train station where he had driven me were: "Don't you let that McLean get you involved in anything."

McLean had a good laugh when I relayed those words to him.

Fourteen

I MEET UP WITH BILL LANG AND SEND OLD MAN FITZSIMMONS OFF TO DREAMLAND

From what I had seen of my future opponent, Peter Felix, I fully expected not to have to do much to beat him and I didn't train at all in preparation for the bout. The fight, which was held on February 19, 1907, was such an easy affair that I would be hard pressed to remember the details. All I remember is that as soon as my man came within striking distance, I let loose a punch on his chin that knocked him out so convincingly that no one had any doubt whatsoever about his condition. I didn't dare look the crowd in the face after that one and only round, but they all seemed to think I had done something wonderful and I wasn't going to try to change their minds. I didn't get much out of that match and Felix got even less, poor boy!

Bill Lang and his friends were sure that he could take me and McLean set up a fight to take place in Melbourne, on March 4. Bill was, in those days, a good second-rate boxer and he put up a very good fight. I did my best to see to it that the crowd got their money's worth and waited until the ninth round to send Bill off to Dreamland. After that, Lang built up a very good record and a few of his friends would have liked me to give him a rematch. I must say that he is an upstanding fellow and one of the most skillful boxers I have ever faced in the ring. I had no one left to fight in Australia. As soon he learned that I was on my way to Sydney, Bill Squires, the Australian heavyweight champion, had ducked my challenge and taken off for America, to fight Tommy Burns. This was a big disappointment for me, but there was nothing I could do but try to laugh about it. I resolved to chase Squires down and force him to fight me.

While I was waiting for the boat, I tried to distract myself a little by betting on the horses. When I left the country, I had won $15,000, enough to keep me from suicide.

When I arrived in California, not without having had another taste of seasickness, I had another unpleasant surprise. I couldn't manage to come to an agreement with Bill Squires. He found more excuses to duck a fight with me than I can tell you. When I saw that he was acting in truly bad faith, I stopped insisting, but I took a strong dislike to him.

On the other hand, I did have one pleasant compensation when I found out that Bob Fitzsimmons was talking about a twenty-round fight with me in the Quaker City. This was a fight I had been dreaming of for years, without ever being able to make it happen. The problem wasn't that Bob was worried about the color question. Oh, no! He was one of the champions who had never been concerned about that ridiculous prejudice.

All the arrangements were made quickly and the match was scheduled for July 17. Although Bob had made the greatest efforts to get back in shape, as soon as I saw him hop into the ring, I realized that he was only a shadow of his former self.

I was eager to go ahead and hit the poor old guy, but the crowd had to get their money's worth. I started jumping around him and turning him around in circles, like a barrel-maker does with a barrel. Every so often I would throw an uppercut, sometimes a jab, but not so much that he couldn't stay on his feet. At the end of the first round, the former champion was so befuddled he could barely smile and open his eyes.

At the beginning of the second round, I started in on a new tactic. The man standing in front of me had won the title by beating the best fighters of his era. He still had the reputation of being one of the most skillful artists of the ring. It wasn't my fault if the public didn't realize that he had nothing going for him but his former glory. If I let him stay on his feet until the end of the sixth round, what would I get out of the bout? It was all well and good to be nice to an old boxer, but I couldn't afford to compromise my reputation and I would have been very foolish to do so.

Having reflected on all that, I landed a roundhouse right on my opponent's jaw, dropping him to the canvas so hard that the referee had only to count to ten for the fight to be over.

The oddest thing about the entire affair was that this knockout earned me a huge leap in everyone's esteem. He knocked out Bob Fitzsimmons! This Johnson must be a real boxer! Nothing could stop me from being a contender for the championship now. This goes to show how reputations are made. For years I had been fighting the best men who ever put on the gloves and all of those bouts put together did less for my reputation than knocking out poor old Bob Fitzsimmons!

At this point, people started realizing that I was worth something. Managers got interested in me and I received a number of offers. But I was thinking only of the championship and was much less concerned about "dough." I wasn't going to be satisfied until I could fight Tommy Burns and all my thoughts were of setting up a match with him. He didn't help me out much in this matter, seeming to be as anxious to avoid me as I was to fight him.

I had always heard it said that John L. Sullivan had a negative opinion of me as a boxer. He didn't want to admit that I was a first-rate man; he was in the habit of criticizing the way I fought and saying that I would never be a champion. After my fight with Fitzsimmons, Sullivan started declaring all over the place that I didn't have a champion's punch and never would. He added that his young sparring partner, Kid Cutler, was better than Jack Johnson and that he was ready to set Cutler up against him.

I had no reason to pay any attention to John's convoluted theories, but he started getting on my nerves, so I proposed to fight his young friend. He agreed, and the bout took place in Reading, Pa., on August 28. To prove to John what a poor prognosticator of boxing matters he was, I saw to it that his young friend got precious little glory out of his match with me. In the very first round, I landed a roundhouse right on his jaw that put him right to sleep. That was the last I ever heard of John L. Sullivan's opinions.

Two weeks later, I had a fight with Sailor Burke in Bridgeport, Conn. It was a six-rounder and the sailor had been advised by Wilson, his manager, to throw himself on the canvas in order to avoid a knockout and get a draw. I was so disgusted by this bout that I decided not to have any more dealings whatsoever with that category of individuals who think that boxing consists of falling down and getting back up. I promised myself that if I won the championship, I would defend it against all comers, but until that time I reserved the right to choose my opponents.

Fifteen

IN PURSUIT OF TOMMY BURNS

I had had five bouts since New Year's Day, four of which I won by knockout, but I hadn't gained very much ground in the esteem of my contemporaries. My win over Fitzsimmons had of course elevated me to the rank of contender for the title of world champion, but all my efforts to fight Tommy Burns, the title-holder, had been in vain. Of all the cunning fellows I have encountered on this earth, Tommy is certainly the most cunning. He won the championship without ever having squared off with the champion but now that the title was his, he wasn't about to let it go without a struggle.

Mr. Jeffries was the one who finagled the whole business of the championship, without anyone ever knowing exactly how it had taken place. When Marvin Hart—who had won a decision over me in San Francisco, in 1905—was matched against Jack Root in Reno, Jeffries was chosen to referee the bout. So he took it upon himself to declare that he would hand over the title of champion to the winner of the bout and retire from the ring. Hart won by knockout and was declared the winner by Jeffries. Burns challenged Hart as soon as he could. He won easily, administering such a thrashing that Hart couldn't get out of bed for several weeks.

The public didn't appreciate Mr. Jeffries' way of doing things, disposing of the championship title like that. Burns was asked to fight Fitzsimmons in a twenty-round match. The contract was signed and $23,000 worth of tickets had already been sold in advance when the police stepped in and forbade the match. Was Burns disappointed? Oh, no! He simply proceeded to go back to

California, where he fought Jim Flynn, the fireman from Pueblo, whom he knocked out in fifteen rounds.

Naturally, Burns reclaimed the title. It was his right to do so, but he didn't get it back right away. Philadelphia Jack O'Brien, who had beat Fitzsimmons, also claimed it as his. The two fought in Los Angeles, with Mr. Jeffries as referee. The bout lasted twenty rounds and ended in a draw. So they had to fight again. But I'll come back to that later.

Since Tommy Burns had fought Jim Flynn in his quest for the championship, everyone said I should do likewise. It wasn't in my best interest to point out that Jim was not in the same class as me and it wasn't anybody else's business to do so. So the match was scheduled for forty-five rounds, in Colma, California, on November 2, 1907. At the beginning of the eleventh round, Jim started looking at me with a smile on his face, saying: "You sure are a pretty nigger, Jack!" A hard straight right to the jaw put an abrupt halt to the string of compliments; he crumbled to the canvas, completely knocked out. It took four minutes to rouse him from his slumber. My fight against Flynn was one of the easiest I had ever had. In the first round, I closed his left eye; after that, I had a superb target at which to aim my favorite left jab.

When Jim was able to open his one good eye, he gave a little speech to his seconds and everyone around him: "The better man won," he said, "and let me tell you, the next man to fight him had better watch out. He's a great fighter and I was completely out of my league with him."

This was absolutely true. Flynn was an excellent little boxer but too small for me. I also took my turn making a speech, because the crowd was clamoring for me. I threw out a challenge to any man who wanted to fight me and announced that I was ready to square off with Tommy Burns. The evening was an excellent one for me. The crowd was large and the gate receipts totaled approximately $7,000.

It was all well and good for me to say that I wanted to fight Tommy Burns, but the problem was that he didn't seem to share my desire in the slightest. To show you how clever the champion was, I return to my account of the way he won the championship.

You will remember that we left things undecided between Jack O'Brien and Tommy, with a second match necessary. The public insisted that they meet in the ring again. And in fact, there was no other way to settle things.

After numerous conversations, the two men came to the following secret agreement: O'Brien agreed to fight Tommy Burns, on the condition that Burns promised to throw the fight. They argued the matter for a long time. Finally, Burns consented to O'Brien's demands.

Now listen to what Burns did. The minute the timekeeper called "Time!" to start the fight, the referee came forward and said that O'Brien had asked Burns to take a dive and that Burns had pretended to accept the proposition, solely so as to force O'Brien into the ring, but had never intended to keep his promise. The referee added that the fight was about to begin and that there was no chance that either of the men was going to take a dive.

At that point, Tommy said something along these lines to Jack:

"This is going to be the only real fight you've ever had in your life. You've bluffed and cheated the fans enough. Now you have a chance to win a fight for real. Give it your all because I'm going to give it mine!"

Then commenced a tough bout that lasted twenty rounds, during which O'Brien absorbed terrible punishment. But what a display of boxing! You see the kind of men I had to fight?

After the O'Brien-Burns affair, when Jeffries had bestowed the title of champion on the winner Burns, Bill Squires made known his intention to challenge the title-holder. He quickly made plans to leave Australia when he learned that I was on my way there. When he got to America, he introduced himself all around as the champion of Australia. He played the part quite well. When he squared off with Tommy Burns, on July 4, he was a ten-to-seven favorite against the new champion. When the bell rang, Squires jumped on Burns like a wild bull. Imagine the surprise of the crowd at ringside when the bout ended two minutes and six seconds later, with Burns as the winner. Indeed, the champion put the Australian to sleep in the first round with one of his favorite punches, a right to the jaw.

Immediately after that fight, Gunner Moir, the champion of England, challenged Burns for the world championship. Burns accepted the challenge and traveled approximately 9,000 miles to fight his opponent in his own country. This was the first heavyweight title fight to take place in England for thirty-seven years. You can imagine the interest it created, especially since national pride was at stake.

Moir was beaten in ten rounds and Burns made $12,000 from the bout. After that, the wily Canadian—his real name is Noah Brusso and he was born of Jewish parents—signed for a fight with Jack Palmer.[1] He should have been ashamed to take money for that bout, because the fight was truly a joke. Palmer had no skill and no power; he was sent to Dreamland in the fourth round. Burns' cut was at least $10,000.

It was while he was in England, collecting purses here and there, being none too particular about the worthiness of his opponents, and happy to put on mere exhibitions, that I learned from a friend of mine that Mr. Burns was in the habit of talking about me in public, in roughly the following fashion:

Good old Jack Johnson is the first man I want to fight when I go home to America, if there is money in it, because he doesn't seem any harder to beat than any of the men I've beaten up to now, like Marvin Hart—who beat Johnson in San Francisco several months before I beat Hart myself. Everybody knows I gave Hart such a beating that he couldn't get out of bed for several days. That just shows what kind of boxer Johnson is. When I signed on to fight Squires in San Francisco, Johnson was there and he asked me if I would want to fight him, if won the fight with Squires. I told him that if there was enough money in it, I would certainly accept.

"I am prepared to put up $10,000," Johnson said.

"Put up or shut up," I replied.

"I've only got $700 on me," he said, "Here it is. If I don't get the rest of the money to you tomorrow, the $700 is yours."

I took him up on his offer and he put the $700 in the hands of a white man, who, I have since learned, was a friend of his. I wrote a check for $10,000. The next day, instead of putting up the rest of his share, Johnson took his $700 back and didn't want to hear any more about the matter. I asked him if he was mocking me, because there were a number of newspapermen there. All he did was flash his big white teeth. So I wanted to show just what kind of a man he was. I proposed that we close the door and fight for sheer honor. But the big boy backed down. At that point, I said things to him the half of which would have gotten me killed by any other man in the world in two minutes flat. All the nigger boxers are of that caliber. If we let them have their way, they would be the only people left on earth. I'm going to go home to America and he's going to have to learn, one way or another, just how hard my fists are.

You can imagine my fury when I was informed of these statements. This was a man my manager Sam Fitzpatrick and I had been pursuing since the day the title of champion was bestowed on him by Mr. Jeffries! A man to whom I had never spoken a word in my life! I told Fitz that I would pursue the damn liar to the ends of the earth and make him eat his words.

My manager agreed with me that that was the best thing to do and we set off for England, where Burns was making his fortune without exerting himself too much. In those days, he was the idol of the English sporting public, who had never seen him beaten and took every word he said as Gospel. Neither my manager nor I had money to burn, but we had got it into our heads that we had to persuade Mr. Burns that he was longing to return to America.

When we got to London, and proposed a match to the world champion, he refused the offer. As you can well imagine, he set things up so as not to appear to be backing down, by demanding the entire purse for himself, win or lose. Sam Fitzpatrick, of course, was unwilling to agree to such unfair terms. Burns' behavior was roundly criticized by the English sportswriters and they let it be understood that he was afraid of me.

Eventually, it got so the Canadian Jew with the Irish ring name could no longer hold his head up.[2] He had to go ahead and choose: either fight me or leave the country. He opted for the latter alternative, abandoning some financially superb propositions in order to put an ocean between us. Sam Fitzpatrick and I put so much pressure on him that he finally consented to consider the matter and scheduled a day and time for the first preliminary discussions. In truth, we were only slightly surprised, when we arrived at the appointment, to learn that the champion had left the day before for Australia, without leaving any message whatsoever. That was Burns all right!

Everyone thought (and I'm not sure Burns himself wouldn't have agreed) that this was very good for us. The English newspapers declared that any chance of a fight between Burns and me was lost and added all sorts of comments that weren't exactly flattering to the world champion. I must say that the English journalists are the most upstanding group of men I have ever encountered. They are incapable of promoting interest in a shady deal, once they have recognized it as such. The general opinion was that Burns was terrified by the idea of finding himself inside the ropes with me and that he had left because he realized that he was going to have his hands full defending his title.

No one thought that Fitzpatrick and I had any intention of following Burns to Australia. We were completely "broke," but we hadn't given up on our idea of chasing after the champion as soon as we could.

A few sportsmen who had befriended me tried to find some boxer who would be willing to fight me. It was difficult. Finally they managed to match me against Ben Taylor. We fought in Plymouth, on July 31. This was my first bout that year, 1908. I knocked the Englishman out in the eighth round. That was enough so that Gunner Moir and all the others wanted nothing to do with me. Luckily, we succeeded in making a little money outside the ring and we bought two first-class tickets to Australia.

I had found out that Burns was going around telling everyone that if we consented to his demands, he was prepared to fight me. Before I got to Australia, I swore to myself that I would either force him to live up to his words or make him eat them. I was still so furious about the story of the fight in a room with no spectators that he claimed to have proposed to me that I decided to let him have all the money if necessary; I would fight for honor. I had gone crazy over the whole thing and Sam Fitzpatrick had gone as crazy as I had.

In Australia, we were finally going to nail Mr. Burns to the wall. Fortunately for us, we were to find a man there who very much wanted to see us fight. That man was Mr. Hugh McIntosh and he had what it took to make the thing happen. He guaranteed $30,000 to Burns if he was willing to fight me, regardless of the outcome. I wanted to fight the champion so badly that I was more than happy to accept $5,000 as my share, if the ticket sales didn't allow for more. This sum didn't even cover the expenditures we had made to chase Burns down, but as I said, I would have agreed to fight for no money and no prize. I was nearing my goal: one more step and I would be there. I was going to get what I had longed for for almost fifteen years!

Burns took a long time thinking over the proposition. He spent so many weeks thinking that everyone began to believe that he was just looking for a way to duck out of it. He made it known how much it would hurt his reputation to get into the ring with a black man and brought up all sorts of objections. But Mr. McIntosh kept after him and eventually he was obligated to accept the terms of his own proposition. There has never been a boxer, before or since, so assured of getting his money!

Sixteen

I AM CHAMPION OF THE WORLD!

There was an explosion of joy among Australians when it was announced that the match had been scheduled. It was to be the first time in many years a heavyweight championship had been held outside the United States and here it was in their own backyard. McIntosh had a huge stadium built that could hold 18,000 spectators. Long before the opening bell rang, all the tickets had been sold and an enormous crowd was waiting outside, clamoring to be let in. The tickets cost between five and fifty dollars. Before I got into the ring, McIntosh told me that the gate receipts were up to something like $175,000.

Although I was supposed to get much of it for myself, I was very happy for Mr. McIntosh, who had played his cards pretty well by offering Burns $30,000. You can be sure that this shrewd Scotsman had always known how things would turn out. He later told me that he had always foreseen that I would win and make him a lot of money. All of Australia was interested in the bout. The mob that was pushing its way into the newly constructed stadium at Rushcutter's Bay included thousands of people who wouldn't see so much as an inch of the ring. Many of them had arrived Christmas night and camped out in the open air. It was summer, but it wasn't very hot and the sky was cloudy.

I couldn't help thinking that even if it was out of the ordinary to fight for the championship the day after Christmas, at least you couldn't have dreamed of better weather for the festivities.

Everyone took a passionate interest in the bout. All the big newspapers devoted entire columns to the two opponents. On the morning of December 28, I read a half-page account of my own story in one of them and learned all sorts of things about Jack Johnson that I had never heard before. This was only the second time that a colored man had fought for the championship. Peter Jackson issued a challenge to John L. Sullivan, but Sullivan wouldn't consent to fight a nigger. After Jeffries had taken Bob Fitzsimmons' scalp, Hank Griffin challenged him for the title, but Jeffries demonstrated in four rounds that Griffin had no right to do so. And now I was going to square off with Jeffries' successor.

The betting on the match was the liveliest ever seen in Australia. Before the fight, Burns was a 7/5 to 3/2 favorite. Thousands of dollars were put down at those odds. Of course Burns and I also made our little bets, though I later learned that the Canadian hadn't ventured too far down that road. After the first two rounds, there was a sudden change in the odds and the people who had failed to wager on me earlier had to pay through the nose to do so.

When we climbed into the ring, Burns was 5 feet 7.25 inches tall and weighed 176 pounds. My height was 6 feet 1.75 inches and my weight 196 pounds. The Canadian had a reach of 74.5 inches; mine was only 72.75. His forearm measured 12 inches, mine 13; his biceps 13.25 inches, mine 14.5. His chest was 40.5 inches around and mine 43.5. Burns was twenty-seven years old and I was thirty.

At 10:42 A.M., I entered the stadium, accompanied by my seconds, Sam Fitzpatrick, Mullins, Unholz, Lang, and Bryant. The crowd gave me a splendid reception and I greeted them with a bow. As I was sitting down, Burns made his appearance, surrounded by his seconds, Keating, O'Keefe, O'Donnell, Burke, and Russell. The crowd received him too with an ovation. I got up, crossed the ring, and went over to his corner to shake his hand. I was very courteous to Tommy that morning. You can't imagine the pleasure it gave me to see him there inside the ropes. At long last, the moment had arrived: I had my man right where I wanted him. He couldn't get away from me any more, although he did still seem eager to argue over every possible detail. But my seconds were just as eager not to let him get away with it.

When he stood up, I saw that he was wearing elastic bandages on his elbows and I asked him to take them off. He came to the middle of the ring and asked why I wanted him to take them off, but I insisted. He refused, saying that he wouldn't fight at all without the bandages. For a moment, I thought that the match was off, but finally his seconds persuaded him to get rid of his elastics. I didn't know what he intended to do with those bandages and I have never found out, but I am sure that he had a purpose in mind for them.

At 11:15, we posed for the movie cameras and it was announced that in case of intervention by the police, Mr. McIntosh, the referee, would immediately declare a winner on points. Then we were ready to fight.

I was so happy and so profoundly convinced that I was going to win that I started joking around with Tommy from the very start. He was madder than a wet hen and as soon as I saw how much it annoyed him, I promised myself that I would keep it up. I realized that he was beat even before the first round was over and you can imagine that it was no secret for Tommy either. After a few preliminary thrusts, I landed a nice uppercut on Burns and the Canadian dropped to the canvas. He stayed down for a count of eight. I saw him motion to his seconds that he was all right, so I kept my guard up. When he got up, he threw himself at me with all his might, but I stopped him with a right hand to the head and he staggered back across the ring. Then he ran at me and landed a right on my chin. I answered with a left to the head, just as the bell rang.

In the second round, Tommy tried to clinch, but I landed a nice right-hand punch on his chin. He turned on his ankle and fell to the canvas. But he got up again right away and we went at it. I kept on hitting him with rights and lefts, to both the body and the head and I noticed at the end of the round that his left eye had started to swell. He became more cautious at that point and stayed on the defensive. I continued joking with him, without giving him time to answer my questions.

"What are you scared of, little boy?" I asked him. "Don't forget we're playing a man's game and men are supposed to enjoy it. Get up and fight like a real man. It won't last much longer, little boy."

This language made Tommy furious and I kept it up; I realized annoying the champion was to my advantage and annoyed he certainly was.

"Come here, little boy!" I would say. Sometimes he was so furious that he took me up on the invitation. When I had stopped him cold, I would laugh: "You shouldn't have done that, old pal, just because I asked you to. What are you waiting for? Why don't you hit me with a right to the body and a left to the jaw, like this, little boy?" And my actions would reflect my words. This behavior drove him insane, like a bull that has just seen a red flag, and he would throw himself at me, striking out with fury.

The fourth round was a real battle. In the center of the ring, I landed a hard right under Tommy's ribs and doubled up on it immediately. Then we hammered away at each other like demons, but without many punches really landing. When the bell rang, we were in a clinch.

In the fifth round, Burns came out very fast, hitting me with a right to the head and rights and lefts to the body. The lack of power in his punches proved to me that Tommy was losing his strength; all I had to do was keep up the same tactics and let the champion tire himself out.

To wake him up a bit, I shook him up at the start of the sixth round, then we fell into a clinch. I broke out of it right away and hit Tommy a dozen or so times under the ribs with my right—not too hard, but just enough so that he could feel the unpleasant sensation of it. He answered with one or two lefts to the stomach, but I barely paid attention to those friendly little smacks. I kept on talking to Burns and the people at ringside, joking. At the end of the round, I gave him a couple of rights to the body that he would have preferred not to receive.

In the seventh round, I started going to work more seriously. I rushed across the ring and threw a series of right hands that weren't exactly like pillows. Burns landed a left to my jaw and I answered with a sledgehammer under his right eye. The champion was blowing like a whale and I saw clearly that I could finish him off, more or less whenever I wanted to. This realization made me so happy that I started joking with the crowd. Tommy tried to play his favorite game of infighting, but I prevented him from doing so by punching him in the ribs; he dropped to the canvas for a few seconds.

When the Canadian got off his stool for the eighth round, he was far from being a "$10,000 beauty." Both his eyes were swollen and he was bleeding from the mouth. When he came out of his corner, I told him that I couldn't stand to see him in such bad shape and that I was going to try to make his face look better. All I did for the rest of the round was sock him in both eyes and on the chin, with rights and lefts, like a blacksmith hits an anvil. By the time the bell rang, even his best friends wouldn't have recognized him as the pretty boy who had jumped so gracefully into the ring just a few minutes before.

"Come here, Tommy! A roundhouse right!" I said to him at the beginning of the ninth round. The little man backed away, calling me a "yellow cur." As far as I remember, there was very little fighting in that round, but lots of talking, especially on my part. In the tenth round, I called on all my skill as a boxer and Tommy tried to do the same, but his punches lacked speed.

When we came face-to-face for the eleventh round, Tommy pointed out to me that I looked tired.

"Oh, a bit," I answered. "And yourself? How do you feel, my boy?"

"I never felt better in my life," he responded through lips so swollen he could barely get the words out. "I see you're sweating a little."

"You're right," I laughed. "I've got so much to do trying to keep from hurting you that I'm starting to get hot."

At that moment, there wasn't a man in the audience who didn't know that Burns was outclassed. When the bell rang, he dropped onto his stool like a rag doll.

He nonetheless stood up for the twelfth round and started taking his medicine like a good little boy. But this time I gave him a big dose of it and it seemed like he was finding it hard to swallow. His jaws were so swollen that I couldn't see where I should hit him.

When the bell for the thirteenth round rang, I told myself it was time to finish things. I had had enough fun for one day, and I thought the crowd had gotten their money's worth. So I unleashed such a shower of blows that Tommy was staggering like a drunkard when the bell rang. During the rest between rounds, I noticed that the police officers were holding a very lively discussion and I thought they wanted to put a stop to the bout. McIntosh went into the champion's corner and started talking to him. I heard him tell Tommy that he was a beaten man. But the stubborn Burns replied that he was not and that he was sure he was going to win.[1] Then McIntosh asked the police not to intervene and the bell for the fourteenth round rang.

At that point, I would have been happy to rest but since everyone else wanted more, I was forced to give it to them. At the bell, I rushed at my opponent. He backed up prudently, but I chased after him and landed a terrific right hand to his head. He fell on the ground and stayed there until the count of eight. Then he got back up, on wobbly legs. I rushed at him to hit him again and put an end to his suffering. But at that very moment the police intervened and stopped the bout. Mr. McIntosh then declared that I was the winner on points.

The decision seemed to satisfy everyone, judging by the noise that broke out when it was announced. At that moment, Jack Johnson was the "only pebble on the beach." No one seemed to remember that Tommy Burns had ever existed. His friends carried him into a car and took him back to his training camp at Darling Point, where the doctor took over. The crowd accompanied me back to Manby, a suburb of Sydney, on the coast, where I had set up house. And those people were making so much noise that I doubt you could have heard a dozen brass bands playing all at once over the racket. Aside from the fact that I was very excited and a little "beat up" looking, I felt as good as I had ever felt in my life.

I was so happy with the work I had just done that I would have agreed to do it for free. My share of the gate came to $15,000.[2] Added to my winnings, that made me the respectable sum of $25,000 to take back to America.[3]

I don't think there was a happier man in all of Australia than Sam Fitzpatrick, my manager. Sam needed the win as much as I did. He hadn't gotten a single break since the good old days of Peter Jackson. Everyone who knew him was happy to see him win. "Hooray for Sam!" I heard someone shout as we were leaving the stadium. "He's going to able to drink wine instead of having beer and cheese in the back of the store."

Sam deserved his good fortune. He had had faith in me when I was anything but a "money maker." He took me to England and paid all my expenses. It was thanks to him, once again, that I was able to make the long trip to Australia. I was as happy about his success in the whole business as I was about my own.

Seventeen

I DEFEND MY TITLE

At last I was champion of the world! Other boxers who became champion have told how they felt when they won the coveted title. As for me, I am completely incapable of describing my sensations. I was happier than you might suppose and even happier than I can say. For fifteen years, I had aspired to that glorious day, all the while certain that I would make it happen. Since the day Joe Choynski showed me the way by knocking me out, I had kept my eyes fixed on the title to be won. Now that the deed was done, I was a little sad to think that I would no longer have to struggle to conquer it. But I consoled myself with the thought that I would have my hands full fighting to hold on to what I had worked so hard to acquire. I had fought more bouts than any man in the world; so many, in fact, that I had lost count of them.

After my fight with Burns, I stayed in Australia until February; during those few months, I had quite a few adventures. I signed a contract with a music hall for $1050 a week. Tommy Burns, when he could appear in public again, was given a better deal: he got $1250 a week, including film rights. We both played to packed houses and made a lot of money for our managers.

Then I got married. I thought I was making enough money at that point to offer myself the luxury of a wife. I had always loved family life, so I decided to take the plunge. My wedding was very simple and I didn't abandon my business interests by going on a honeymoon.[1]

It was around this time that the American and English newspapers began telling all sorts of stories about what I was doing in Melbourne. They reported that I had been treated as a charity case in the municipal hospital, that I had claimed to be penniless and unable to pay for my care. Nothing was farther from the truth than this story. How would I have been able to claim to be indigent when I came to the hospital every day in my own automobile!

Here's what really happened: I had a bit of a sore throat and figured I would be best cared for in a hospital. It was a free hospital and I didn't know that they weren't going to ask me to pay for the treatment I received. I offered to pay the doctor who had taken care of me but he wouldn't accept anything. So I had a dozen pairs of silk socks sent to him, as a token of my gratitude, but he refused those as well.

The truth is, Australia made a fair amount of money off me. I had to pay income tax on all the money I earned; furthermore, I made numerous gifts to various charitable causes throughout the time I was in the country. That's the true story of what happened at the hospital.

Our return trip on the *Mukura* was very pleasant from all points of view. We had good weather and I suffered only a little bit of seasickness. Several concerts were organized on board in which I participated, playing some pieces on the cello, accompanied by Mrs. Johnson at the piano. Our participation was much appreciated by the passengers and the proceeds, which went to a charity (I can't remember which one), reflected that fact.

It was during this crossing that Mr. Fitzpatrick and I broke off relations. It is not necessary for me to go into the details of this rupture but I would like to make clear that it entailed nothing for Fitzpatrick to be offended by. I realized that I no longer required his services but we had absolutely no unpleasant conversations on the subject. He had rendered me considerable service in helping me to chase Burns down and force him to fight; although he had been compensated for his efforts, I was nonetheless grateful to him. Everything that was said in the newspapers about a dispute between the two of us is thus completely inaccurate.

When I arrived in Victoria, BC, on March 9, an opportunity to defend my title awaited me. A big boy named Victor McLaglen was anxiously waiting in Vancouver for the chance to show the world that the new champion was a phony. The day after I landed, I fought him: six rounds sufficed to prove that his name might have been Victor but he was not victorious.

As I got off the boat in Vancouver, representatives from all the big newspapers were there to meet me; from all sides, they asked the same question: "Have you made up your mind to fight Jeffries?"

This was the gist of my answer:

Sure, I am ready to fight Jeffries—to fight any man in the world who challenges me. And they'll have to throw me out of the ring to beat me. It annoys me to hear people call Jeffries the champion. Why do they do that? When a congressman isn't reelected by his constituents, when a mayor resigns, they're just "Mr. Ex-Congressman" or "Mr. Ex-Mayor." Why should someone remain champion when he quit the ring the way Jeffries did? An ex-champion, that's what he is. Now if Mr. Jeffries wants to get his title back, if he thinks he can, I'm ready to square off with him.

And another thing, gentlemen: why are you so concerned with Jeffries' demands? I'm the champion, not him. So you should be paying attention to my demands. I want a purse split between the winner and the loser. I'm not worried about the percentages, whether it's 60/40 or 75/25—that's a matter to be settled later on by our managers. That's how it was when I fought Burns. I chased him all over the world, all the way to Sydney. If Jeffries wants to fight me, he's a big enough boy to say so himself.

Besides, I could do without other people now. If the match was going to take place, though, I preferred that it not be right away. I had some very attractive offers in various theaters and I preferred to go on tour and make some money before I went back to training. But it was ordained that things would not stay quiet for me for long. Before long I had to fight Mr. Joseph Francis Aloysius Hagan.

This gentleman, better known by the name Philadelphia Jack O'Brien, his ring name, had already had the pleasure of fighting a world champion and had not lost all hope of winning the title. I could hardly blame him. I myself had been a title seeker, not the titleholder, just a short while before I agreed to square off with him in his own city of Philadelphia, on May 15, 1909.

Eighteen

THE BOXER AS MAN OF THE WORLD

Of all the men I met up with in the ring, it had always seemed to me that O'Brien had the most interesting career. I always had great respect for the man who, with no experience other than what he had acquired as Kid McCoy's sparring partner, went to England and stayed for a year, during which he beat the best men that country had to offer. Some of his finest performances on the other side of the water came when he knocked out George Crisp, the champion of England, in eleven rounds, and when he put Dido Plumb, the middleweight champion, to sleep. When he came back here, O'Brien only wanted to fight heavyweights.

But what I always admired about Jack was the effort he made to seem like a born gentleman; his natural refinement would be the envy of the most elegant dandies of Philadelphia and elsewhere. And his mansion! When he had scraped together enough money to buy himself a house, don't think for a second that he chose one on some side street. He bought a lot in the neighborhood where the Quaker City's equivalent of the "Four Hundred" lived, right next door to the dean of the university.

It was a genuine pleasure for me to fight that man. The purse was not attractive. Mr. Harry D. Edwards, manager of the National Athletic Club, which had promoted the fight, offered me a guarantee of $5,000 and paid my travel expenses. This was not a great deal for a man who had returned from Australia with $25,000 in his pocket, but I considered the pleasure of fighting Jack O'Brien to be very valuable. O'Brien worked on a percentage basis,

30 percent of the gate. His share turned out to be $6,000 and the event brought in more than $10,000 to the club. The clubmen of Philadelphia are skillful businessmen!

It was a nice little exhibition and no one protested when, at the end of the sixth round, the referee announced that he could declare "no decision" without running the risk of hurting anyone's feelings.

As I was climbing into a car to go to the National Athletic Club for my six-round no-decision bout against Jack O'Brien on a beautiful May evening, my wife called out from the window of our hotel room, "Now there are two Jacks who give you a reason to celebrate the month of May!" I wasn't entirely sure what she meant by that, but figured that it must be something quite good. I just waved at her, with my hat in my hand, and left.

I had a very good feeling about the kind of fight we were going to have. The man across the ring from me was probably the most skillful and most knowledgeable boxer in the world. He was also a puncher, but it was mostly by skill that he won his matches. The best I could hope for was to surprise him, when he least expected it, with one of my favorite punches. But I admit that it seemed like that would be very hard to do in six rounds.

When he entered the ring, I couldn't help admiring my little opponent. I walked up to him and shook both his hands, congratulating him. He was the first American ever to win the championship of England. John C. Heenan, you will remember, only got a draw against Tom Sayers, since the bout was stopped. The same thing happened to John L. Sullivan against Charley Mitchell and Jake Kilrain against Jim Smith. Jack was also the smallest man to fight for the title of world champion since Jem Mace, the gypsy, who held it from 1861 to 1862. The more I looked at him, the more amazed I was that a little puppet of a boxer like that had dared square off against formidable giants and had managed to knock out the marvelous Bob Fitzsimmons.

Jack was only five feet, ten inches tall in boxing shoes. I looked him over carefully and found him to be in good shape, with plenty still going for him. He had a fine boxer's body, short and thick, perched on top of a pair of long, round, not-too-heavy legs. His chest was broad but his shoulders and arms weren't very strong. Nothing about him indicated great strength but he seemed quick as a cat. His overall musculature was the most elegant you can imagine. His face was square, with a heavy jaw, a prominent chin, and the light-colored eyes of a man who is not easily duped. I saw right away that I would have in him a very handsome, but very tough, opponent.

The first conclusion I drew from all this was that I wouldn't be able to take care of him in six rounds. I calculated that I would need at least ten to get the job done. He reminded me of those little drops of mercury that you roll around on a table: when you try to pick them up with your fingers, they're already gone. The same was true of Jack O'Brien; that's how hard it was to put him on the canvas.

When we shook hands in the center of the ring, he was so elegant, looked so stylish, and behaved so graciously that I almost apologized for not being in a tuxedo. We were the same age, thirty-one, but we hardly looked like twins. If I had been told at that moment, as I was to learn later, that my opponent had just dined at the home of the famous banker A. J. Drexel Biddle, I would have been rather amazed.

I forgot to tell you that while we were putting on the gloves, someone read aloud a telegram from San Francisco, in which Bill Delaney issued a challenge to me on behalf of Al Kaufmann, offering to bet $10,000 on a fight between the two of us, to be held after the one I had signed for with Stanley Ketchel, set for October 12, 1909. Delaney added that he challenged both of us, Ketchel and me, to fight his boy within the space of six days, the entire purse to go to the winner. This was very pleasant news for me and I just laughed and laughed, unable to stop myself.

I started off fast, forcing O'Brien into the ropes. He got me in a clinch and doubled up on my nose. I answered with a left to the stomach that sent him to the canvas, but he only stayed there for two seconds. He landed two light left hands to the face; I stood still, laughing, and waited for him to do it again. Finally, I hit him with a hard left to the face and doubled up on it. At that point the little man started taking liberties with my mouth that I would never have expected from such a well-mannered person.

I began the second round with two rights to the body, but the referee didn't seem pleased by my bothering his little friend and I was invited not to do it again. I noticed that the spectators didn't approve of the way I was hitting their esteemed fellow citizen either. From that moment on, we played a very gentle little game. In the fourth round, however, I was close to bringing the fight to a close; I landed a right to my opponent's body and put him on the ground. But he got up right away and hit me in the face with a left. At the sound of the bell, we were in a clinch. In the fifth round, O'Brien landed a left to my nose and I sent him to the canvas. After that, I landed two lefts, one to the heart, and one to the jaw. The crowd was starting to make known that I was hitting their little favorite too hard and threatened me if I didn't change my tactics. I had no desire to be disqualified and we continued to exchange caresses.

I knew then that I would never be able to take my man out in the allotted time. Since there would be no decision on points, the result was going to mean nothing, in spite of the fact that I was quite sure of winning the bout. The crowd was on O'Brien's side from start to finish. And although the color line had no influence here, Phil-Jack was nonetheless the crowd favorite. Any referee with the courage to declare that I had outclassed Philadelphia Jack on that fine May evening would surely have had a surly crowd on his hands.

At the start of the sixth and final round, we shook hands and immediately went into a clinch. I landed a left hand to the face and a right to the chest. Jack didn't want to give me any more chances to hit him and he started running around the ring, with me running after him. When I was able to catch up with him, I landed a left to the face and a right uppercut to the chin.

I had him then and I would have happily given up my $5,000 purse to have the match go two more rounds. But that was not to be. We exchanged a few more love taps before the bell, then the referee declared the match over.

I don't think I've ever come out of a fight having taken as few punches as I did with Jack. On the other hand, I'm sure he stayed in bed for at least a day or two, which didn't prevent the crowd from giving their favorite an ovation that I wouldn't have thought the people of Philadelphia capable of. I felt truly guilty about having treated little Jack so roughly.

On the way back to the hotel, I told someone that I hoped the bout wouldn't do any harm to Jack's social standing. He just laughed and told me this little story.

Shortly after Jack and his family had moved into their splendid new house, the man telling me the story went to call on them. Jack gave him a tour of the house, from top to bottom, pointing out to him all its wonders. As the guest was leaving and the two of them were standing on the doorstep, he said to the boxer: "It looks like you have some fine neighbors, Mr. Hagan."

"Oh, very fine," Jack replied, in a dignified tone. "Over there is Mr. Drexel's house—the banker, don't you know, really a very fine person. The house on this side belongs to his son-in-law and this one here to the dean of the University of Pennsylvania. Very respectable people, every one of them, and I've never had any grounds for complaint."

The man telling me the story thought that it was a joke, but I am convinced that Jack was speaking in all seriousness. I told my wife the story and she thought it was very funny, too.

Here is another story that proves that Jack really does belong to high society. When he bought his house, he sent out more than two hundred dinner invitations to the most eminent men in the city and they all showed up. If that's not proof, I don't want to hear any more about it. Personally, I think Jack brings honor to his profession and I still regard my fight with him, on that lovely May evening, as one of the most pleasant episodes of my professional career. I was pleased to find out that he had succeeded in his affairs. They say he owns twenty-one houses in Philadelphia and that he has a bank account from which he can draw a check for $100,000 at any time, without any trouble whatsoever. No wonder he's a member of high society.

Nineteen

STANLEY KETCHEL'S TERRIFIC RIGHT!

After I fought the Italian boxer Tony Ross, in a six-round match in Pittsburgh on June 30, 1909, I crossed the continent to show Billy Delaney that his latest discovery, Al Kaufmann, was not in the same league with me. To this day, Billy has created more champions than any other man on earth, and when he makes it known that he has come across the raw materials with which to construct a new one, everybody sits up and takes notice.

I knew personally what Billy's most recent protégé was worth, because I had been there when he couldn't stop Tony Ross from lasting ten rounds with him in their last fight, at the Fairmount Athletic Club in New York. This was certainly one of the funniest fights I have ever attended. Even now, when I think about it, I laugh so hard my jaw almost falls off.

Tony was as fat as a prize pig at a county fair. The way the Italian, who looked more like a dropsy patient than a boxer, took Billy's handsome young man to task was a joy to behold. Not only did he last ten rounds against Kaufmann, he almost took the Californian out in the fifth. I wish you could have seen Billy Delaney's face during that fifth round. He looked like he was being operated on by a first-year dental student. Tony had completely taken his boy apart and was setting him up for the punch that would send him to Dreamland. It was only the Italian's snail-like slowness that saved Kaufmann. That boy sure moved slow! Kaufmann had all the time he needed to come to before Tony could finish him off; then he rushed at the Italian and gave him a terrible beating. I've never seen anything so funny in my life.

Before the fight was over, I was ready to bet all my hard-earned money that Billy Delaney had made a mistake this time. If he wanted a new heavyweight champion in the mold of his two great protégés, Jim Corbett and Jim Jeffries, he would do well to choose someone other than the handsome young boy who was in the process of beating up poor Tony. All things considered, though, the Italian put up a good fight. He was certainly a puncher and I didn't waste my money that night attending that innocent bit of fun. Fat as a pig, with rolls of flesh all over his body, Tony was able to hold on for those ten rounds only because he had the courage of a bulldog and the spine of a Texas mule. There was blood everywhere; it looked like a dogfight. Talk about Roman gladiators! I would never have thought until that night that a man's body had so much blood in it.

It was his own poor conditioning, not his opponent's blows that beat Tony. I think he could easily have beat Kaufmann if he had sufficiently and appropriately trained for the fight. Kaufmann, on the other hand, was too tired to beat Tony in the second half of the match. Ten weeks later, when I had some fun with Tony in a six-round no-decision match in Pittsburgh, I found him better trained, in better condition, and able to do much better work. Although I won every round, he certainly lasted all six. In my fight with Al Kaufmann, I think I convinced everyone watching that my opponent was not in my league. He's a brave, good-looking boy, but if he thinks he can become a champion, I feel sorry for him.

On the afternoon of October 16, as I was on my way to my car to drive myself to the Colma stadium to fight Stanley Ketchel, I ran into a friend of mine, who stopped me to give me a little piece of advice.

"You'd do well to pay attention to that terrible roundhouse right of Stanley's," he told me. "It's really the only hard punch he can land."

I burst out laughing and replied, "Thanks for the information but that little boy is going to be like a poodle up against a greyhound in that ring with me."

And that's exactly how it was. I played with the kid for eleven rounds[1] and then put him to sleep with such a flurry of punches that the leather of my glove was completely torn up by all the contact it had with the middleweight champion's teeth.

When Stanley fell, he was stretched out on the canvas, flat on his back, with his arms stretched out in the shape of a cross. I saw that he was as inanimate as a piece of wood and I was stricken by the fear of having killed him. I couldn't take my eyes off him while the referee counted him out, and when it was over and his seconds picked the fellow from Michigan up to carry him to his corner, I followed every move with an anxious heart. How happy I was when I saw Stanley start giving signs that he was about to come back from Dreamland!

Since Stanley dared to imagine that the title of champion could be his, I dare to say that he never had the slightest chance against an old hand like me. During the fight, the crowd made it sufficiently clear that all their sympathy was for the white man. There was applause for him every time he did something that even looked like an attack, whether it amounted to anything or not, but there was none for me, even when I picked him up off the canvas in the middle of a round and put him back on his feet.

In those days, Ketchel didn't know much more about boxing than I did when I had fought Joe Choynski nine years earlier. He threw good punches and had some power but he couldn't begin to get them past the guard of an experienced boxer, a man who knew how to block and counter.

The sportswriters criticized Ketchel for not having attacked enough, for not having harassed me. They claimed that he would have made a better showing if he had. Personally, I figure that it wouldn't have done him much good. I think, on the contrary, that Stanley had read what Burns had done against me in Australia and tried to make his reading pay off.

I picked up $53,000 in all for the fight with Stanley Ketchel. The purse was $33,000 and I got $20,000 worth of the proceeds from the film.

When I received the pleasing total of $53,000, I wondered if I was prouder of that pretty little wad than I had been of the ten cents and pair of red socks that the milkman used to give me every Saturday, twenty years earlier, in Galveston. As far as I can remember, I think the scales tipped in favor of the $53,000. But I'll never forget those red socks!

Twenty

MR. JEFFRIES' PRETENSIONS

Although I had succeeded in satisfying my ambition to become champion of the world, and now had a bigger fortune than I had ever dreamed of, I still wasn't entirely satisfied. I had traveled all over the world and had had a taste of all the good things in life. I had put aside thousands of dollars, had housed all the members of my family, sent my young brothers and sisters to school, and given my dear old mother a fine house in Chicago.

Perhaps I could have declared myself satisfied after all that, but that was impossible. I thought all the time about the fact that I had something else to do before I could rest and live the easy life. I made up my mind to do it or die trying.

You have perhaps not forgotten that the primary reason I chased down Tommy Burns was not to take the title away from him—of course that was a small factor—but to clear up the story he had been telling that I was afraid to fight him when he insulted me. Well then! There was another man, Mr. James J. Jeffries, the former champion, who had said the same thing about me. I had never given a fig about what the ex-champion might have had to say about the "color line." No one can please everyone and his brother, and I respect the opinions of any honest man. I had devoted sixteen years of my life to the noble art and I couldn't remember a single occasion when Jack Johnson had tried to take a seat that hadn't been offered to him or force his way into a group of whites.

Naturally, I myself didn't respect the "color line." One of my sparring partners used to cite these lines:

For there is neither east nor west,
Border nor breed nor birth.
When two strong men stand face to face,
Though they come from the ends of the earth.

No, I would never have quarreled with Mr. Jeffries over his hesitation to fight a black man. My desire to square off with him was due to another cause altogether.

Like Tommy Burns, he had spread rumors all over the country, rumors so closely resembling the Canadian's that I strongly suspected Jeffries of having borrowed them from him. They were all intended to give a dim view of my personal courage, to portray me as a coward. Furthermore, these rumors were later published in Jeffries' memoirs, written by Bob Edgreen of the *New York Herald*, since Jim is somewhat lacking in the literacy department. I excerpt here the passage from his pseudoautobiography that has to do with the matter:

Several amusing things happened while I was out of the ring. Jack Johnson, the black fighter, didn't amount to enough when I retired to be considered as an opponent. No promoter would have put up a purse for a fight between us. But now that I had been out for a while, and nobody thought there was a possible chance of my fighting again, he began challenging and making a lot of noise. One day I was standing in Harry Corbett's place in San Francisco when in came Johnson with his manager, Zeke Abrahams.

I accused Johnson of challenging me to get advertising.

"Ah really want to fight yo', Misto Jeff," said Johnson.

"You really want to fight, do you?" I asked.

"I shore do," said the black man.

I pulled out a roll of bills and counted it, then turned to Harry Corbett and asked him for all the money he had in the till. He turned around and got it out. The wad totaled up $2,500.

Johnson must have thought I intended to post a forfeit. But I turned around and said: "Here's $2,500. I'll hand it to your own manager to hold. You and I will go right down into the cellar—all alone—see? In the cellar—all alone. We can go there without a permit. If you come up first you get the roll. If I come up first I'll give you $1,000 for hospital expenses. Come on."

Here I started for the cellar. But Johnson just stood still and looked at me with his eyes popped out.

"Dear Misto Jeffries," he said, "I ain't no cellar fighter. I want to fight in public, with a referee. I don't want to fight in no cellar."

"Oh, you aren't even a four-flush," I said. "You're a three-flush."

Johnson and his manager walked away sadly, and as soon as they were gone Harry and I laughed so hard we nearly fell down.

It was a good joke, of course, and it stopped Johnson's bothering me for a while. But he was right. The place to fight was in the ring and not in a cellar.[1]

Now after what happened on July 4 in Reno, do you agree with the great man that the most appropriate place for him to meet up with me was a boxing ring? Don't you think it would in fact have been better for him to fight me in a cave, where there wouldn't have been so many witnesses to the terrible beating I inflicted on him?

All kidding aside, this was the reason why I wanted to fight the ex-champion. As was the case with Tommy Burns, I had been portrayed in a bad light in front of the public and I wanted to prove that I wasn't the man I had been made out to be. Even if I hadn't made one cent from that fight in Reno, the satisfaction of getting my revenge would have been enough. If I could have made do with a battle of words, I might have responded to Jim that on the contrary, he was the one who was afraid to fight me.

Bill Squires had come from Australia to fight Jeffries, and Billy Delaney, Jim's manager and agent at that time, signed for a match. Who backed down on that occasion? Squires was a joker, of course, but the ex-champion was the one who refused to fight. Bill Delaney was so disgusted by the affair that he broke off his association with Jeffries on the spot. As for me, I'm not saying that the great man was afraid to fight Squires. But I thought I stood a better chance than Squires and, in fact, I did.

When I got back from Australia with the title that I had just taken away from Tommy Burns in Sydney, I realized it was only a matter of time before Jeffries rethought his exile from the ring and agreed to square off with me. Every sporting paper in the country started begging the ex-champion to come out of retirement and defend the supremacy of the white race. That issue was of little interest to me and probably to Jeffries too; what was important to him was conserving his reputation as a boxer and a drawing card.

Eventually, it was his good friends among the American public that forced him to accept the fight. I am certain that nothing on earth could have been as unappealing to him but there was nothing else he could do. His friends kept persuading him that he was the only man who could stand up to me; the popular belief was that he would even throw me out of the ring. The following lines, which I excerpt from his memoirs, are truly tragic at this point:

> As for myself, there was no reason for my fighting again. I had a good home, many friends, a good business, everything a man could want. And I had been out of the ring for over five years. Billy Delaney had told me, I remember, that no champion could stay out of the ring for more than two years and come back at his best. I knew that I was in no condition to fight now. I had taken on weight and had lost the old ambition that a great champion must have. But the pressure became too great. I announced that I'd work and when I knew I could be the old Jim Jeffries again I'd fight, and if I couldn't I wouldn't fight for love or money.[2]

The time came when he believed he had become the Jim Jeffries of yesteryear again. He went on a long theatrical tour all across the country, which made him a lot of money. Convinced of having regained his former worthiness, he agreed to risk the fight.

Twenty-One

THE FIGHT OF MY LIFE

I never believed for a minute that the honor of convincing Jeffries to fight would fall to me. I knew perfectly well that nothing I personally could do would bring the great man around to signing a contract with me. It was the public who took charge of the situation and I owe them my gratitude for having brought about what I had been awaiting for so long.

Even before I won the title of heavyweight champion, the word had started going around: all over the country, people were begging Jeffries to save the honor of the white race by bringing the championship back to them. This was an emotional matter, and Jeffries knew that better than anyone, but emotions were of little concern to the ex-champion. With me, things would have been entirely different. I have a romantic temperament and the idea of being the champion of an entire race would have had quite an effect on me.

But no consideration that couldn't be translated into dollars and cents (and a considerable number of them at that) would have any influence on Jeffries. He would have lost very little sleep over the question of saving the honor of the white race if his hand hadn't been forced by public opinion. Before sundown on that December 26, 1908, when I had the honor of scalping Tommy Burns in Sydney, the promoter of the fight, Mr. Hugh McIntosh, had sent a wire to America, offering a purse of $50,000 to Jeffries to fight the winner. At the time that seemed like a substantial offer but when the gate receipts for the fight in Sydney were announced, it seemed less good. Every-one realized that a match-up between the former boilermaker and me could make twice that amount of money. Jeffries' demands increased by the same proportion.

All over the world, savvy people began to doubt that the negotiations would come to fruition. It's fairly easy to see why this was far from an attractive proposition for Jeffries. He hadn't put on the gloves—except on the stage of a theater—for almost six years. He said at first that he didn't see any reason why he should be the one responsible for saving white people's honor. When it was pointed out to him that the title must be won back and that there was no way around it, he replied that Corbett was the man for the job. He added that Corbett would easily be able to beat me. But the public didn't agree with Jeffries; people everywhere were saying that there was only one man able to take on such a task and that his name was James J. Jeffries.

All of this is ancient history, but I bring it up to show how everyone conspired to bring about the solution that I had wanted for so long. All the newspapers joined in the campaign and every day interviews with the former champion were published. But he continued to refuse the very idea of a fight! Oh, my friends, what publicity the eminent Mr. Jeffries got out of the whole affair! All of this made him into a better attraction than ever; it was because of the pressure exerted by this campaign that he signed a contract to appear in vaudeville, for twenty weeks at $2,500 a week. That was how I myself put money in Jeffries' pockets.

This was going on in January 1909.[1] Jeffries made his way to New York to begin his theatrical tour. At each stop along the way, he was besieged by reporters who had come to ask if he still intended to fight me. It was then that he changed his way of answering the question and declared that he might, if he could get back in shape. That seemed to encourage the newspapermen, who started saying that the great champion would fight Johnson as soon as he had finished his theatrical tour. All these rumors gave me a good laugh, because I sensed that the moment was coming when Jeffries would be forced to agree to the fight. Promoters came flocking and we received offers of purses ranging from $50,000 to $200,000 from every big city in the country and even a few from across the ocean. I think I got an offer every other day.

Eventually, things heated up so much that Jeffries announced that he was going to Carlsbad, Germany, to take the waters. That's where all the crowned heads of Europe go to rest up from the fatigue of power and there Jeffries underwent the best treatment his money could buy. He said that if the waters at Carlsbad got him back in shape, he would be ready to fight me. That was fine by me and I prayed every day that his stay at Carlsbad would be beneficial to him.

While Jeff was taking care of himself in Germany, his manager Sam Berger and I met in Chicago and signed a contract for the bout. A couple of days later, I saw a report in the papers that Jeff was having none of it and that Sam Berger had no authority to make transactions on his behalf. That didn't worry me much, since I knew full well that everything would work out in the end.

When he had gotten everything he could hope for out of Carlsbad, Jeffries went to Paris, which was probably more to his taste. I really can't blame him. During his stay in France, he claimed that he was ready to fight me, as long as the purse was at least $10,000. Finally, while crossing back to America, he sent a wireless to a New York newspaper announcing that he was ready for the match. Jeffries arrived in October and began training in a private gym in New York City the very next week.

He tried to keep secret where he was training, but you'd have had to be crazy to think that everyone wasn't going to know as of the next day. Promoters started showing up from all over the place with offers. One of the biggest was from Jack Gleason, from Frisco. He offered $75,000 if the bout was held in that city. I was in Chicago, but I received letters from all over. I finally went to New York with my manager, George Little, and Jeffries and I agreed to meet in a hotel to discuss the conditions for the fight. In addition to Jeffries and me and our respective managers, a number of sportsmen attended this meeting. It was agreed that a bout between us, for the heavyweight championship of the world, would take place, and that the promotion would be handled by the club or person offering the best pecuniary conditions.

I must admit that Jeffries is one of the best businessmen I have ever seen. At this meeting, he had the splendid idea of advising that we wait a while before accepting an offer for the bout. It was October and we decided not to start taking offers until December 1. The most important question to be resolved was that of the city in which the bout would take place. Offers began streaming in from all over: Seattle, Oklahoma, San Francisco, Los Angeles, Paris, and of course Australia. Battling Nelson offered $85,000 to promote the bout in Virginia City, Nevada, and a committee proposed $140,000 for Nampa, Idaho.

It had been decided that the bidding would open at Madison Square Garden, at the same time as an athletic event. But the police intervened, saying that it was a violation of the law forbidding prizefights in the city. So we went over to Hoboken, New Jersey, just on the other side of the Hudson, and the bidding was opened in a hotel. There were a large number of bids. The largest was an offer of $125,000, for a forty-five-round match in California. This offer was made by James Coffroth and John T. Gleason, two rival promoters who had joined forces. They stipulated that they would reserve the film rights for themselves.

There were so many offers (and so much diversity among them) that the bidding had to be extended for two days. Gleason teamed up with Tex Rickard and made another offer, by far the best one of all: $101,000, which would be made up of cash up front and two-thirds of the film proceeds. We could count on the winner's purse being close to $200,000! A tidy sum for a man who would have fought for free and would have even agreed to pay his own expenses.

Twenty-Two

WHO WILL BE THE WINNER?

If I had paid attention to the opinion generally being put forth about the outcome of the fight with Jeffries, I would have ended up doubting myself. As soon as the match was agreed upon, everyone had a good time trying to predict the winner. I must admit that I was very rarely the one they chose. There were very few men competent enough to choose me and those who did think that way were careful not to let their opinion be too widely known. What everyone went around repeating was that Jeff was going to restore the honor of the white race.

For once, I was not in agreement with public opinion. I was full of confidence in Jack Johnson and with excellent reason. I had learned a thing or two during my long career in the ring and I thought I was capable of making as good a prediction as anyone else. I had studied the situation very carefully and didn't see any way that I would not get the better of the ex-champion.

First of all, let's look at the precedents. I was fairly familiar with the history of boxing; in fact, it's the only part of history that has ever interested me. Now there is only one case in which a great boxer was able to get back into his previous condition after having retired from the ring. This was Joe Gans, the colored lightweight from Baltimore. Joe was knocked out by Terry McGovern, in Chicago, on December 13—unlucky number for poor Joe—in the year 1900. A few years later, he climbed back into the ring and won his title back, beating all the best men in his weight class in America, until he in turn was beat by Battling Nelson, who knocked him out twice, on July 4 and

September 29, 1908. Besides, I don't know whether Joe really did everything he might have not to get sent to Dreamland by Terry McGovern in the second round of their fight.

On the other hand, the history of boxing is crawling with anecdotes similar to the story of what ended up happening to Jeffries in Reno. I did everything I could to add his name to the already long list of those who had never been able to be their old selves again in the ring. The example that came to my mind most often was Young Corbett. He was the first to knock out Terry McGovern, managing to do that in the second round, but later, although his did his best to get back in condition, he got beat by everybody. Battling Nelson, Philadelphia Jack O'Brien, Joe Walcott, George Dixon, and Tommy Burns—none of them were ever able to relive their glory days. And in nearly every case, it was their prolonged absence from the ring that was the cause of their downfall.

I never thought for a second that Jeffries would regain anything like his former condition. I had studied him closely in his athletic exhibitions; the audience applauded and cheered for him but I thought he was clearly in bad shape. An ordinary observer doesn't realize what kind of shape a boxer needs to be in. A big pile of flesh and muscles, shown off to its best advantage in the footlights, is impressive to an audience, but a connoisseur has no such illusions.

And so it is hard to explain, if they were in fact pronounced in good faith, the opinions put forth by certain supposedly competent people. Just before the bout, Sam Berger, who otherwise seemed quite well informed on the subject of boxing, gave the following interview to the newspapermen who had come to Reno to attend the fight: "Jeffries has never been one ounce better than he is right now. I don't think Johnson can beat him and the longer the fight goes on, the better Jeffries' chances are."

Doesn't that sound like the prediction of a politician? It is only fair to point out that Sam was Jim's manager, but where was his astute judgment on that occasion?

Roger Conell, Jeffries' head trainer, seemed to believe that he had turned his man into a perfect fighting machine. He amused the reporters with stories like this one:

> In my estimation, Jeffries could not possibly be in better physical condition than he is right now. He got there by a systematic method of training that is new to the art of boxing. How many rounds will the fight last? That doesn't matter. Jeff will be every bit as fast at the end of the thirtieth round as he was in the first. I believe he will outclass Johnson, he will beat him, he will crush him.

The funniest opinion on the subject of the ex-champion's condition came from my old friend Joe Choynski, a man whose opinions concerning fighting matters I had always held in the highest esteem, ever since he knocked me out many years before in Galveston. If I had heard Joe singing this pretty little ditty, I think I would have really been shook up:

> I have never seen an athlete as perfectly prepared as Jeffries. If there is a weak spot in his physical condition, it will only come out in the bout itself, because the man is certainly remarkably well trained. I boxed both Jeffries and Johnson when they were novices. Johnson will be able to do nothing against a man faster, more skilled and more powerful than himself and I would be surprised if the bout lasted more than seven rounds.

Joe must have been as surprised at the outcome as I was when he put me to sleep and as we both were when, on waking up, I realized we were in jail.

All of this served to encourage the ex-champion, to build up his confidence and convince him that he was going to raise the flag of the white race once again. Personally, when I was asked my opinion about who would be the winner of the bout, I gave it without hesitation. The only name that passed my lips was Jack Johnson.

Jack Jeffries, the brother and sparring partner of the ex-champion, thought his opinion was superior to everyone else's, saying:

> Jim is a very careful boxer. That's why I think the bout will last ten rounds or so. One or two hard punches might turn the tide in his favor a little sooner. I lasted eight rounds against Johnson myself and I couldn't hold up half a round against Jim if he went after me for real.

I could have asked Jack if he didn't think that I had made some progress since that long-ago day when we fought or if, by chance, he had done the opposite.

If Bob Armstrong, one of Jeffries' trainers, and a man of my own race, hadn't been employed by the other side, he would have avoided putting forth an opinion as ridiculous as the following:

> If Jack Johnson decides to fight Jeffries, it won't take the great champion long to put him away. If Johnson stays on the defensive, it will only postpone the moment of his fall. I know personally that Johnson will be terrified when he climbs into the ring.

It is interesting to contrast this ridiculous opinion, devoid of all basis in reality, with the opinion of my head trainer Sig Hart, the bantamweight boxer, as he gave it to the newspapermen in Reno, the morning of the bout:

> Johnson will win between the twelfth and eighteenth rounds. We too have our plan and I am sure that the champion will send Mr. Jeffries to the canvas, where he will stay for some time.

This was the opinion of a man who knew both opponents well and was not a blowhard like the others. I have gone into all these details because I don't want the public to think that I doubted for one second that I would take care of the champion, as I in fact did. I don't want anyone to think that I was afraid of Mr. Jeffries or that I was uncertain about the outcome of our fight. The fact that he had too much confidence in his own valor and too much disdain for me is another matter. You will perhaps be surprised that I never reminded him of the stories he and Tommy Burns, with a few variations, had been telling about my personal courage. I didn't do it but don't go thinking it was because I had forgotten either one of those tales.

Twenty-Three

I BEGIN TRAINING

As soon as the contract was signed, Jeffries immediately began training. I, on the other hand, waited until May 9 to get to work.[1] I was in no rush to train too hard, since I was afraid of showing up tired on the day of the fight if I started training too early. There was a lot of talk all over the country about how little interest I was taking in my work; even members of my own entourage reproached me for it. So I decided to calm the worries by beginning to do a few little exercises. I started with some roadwork, inviting all my young friends to join me on a walk of a dozen or so miles. That seemed a bit tough to them and Marty Cutler gave up before we had covered two-thirds of the distance.

In the afternoon, I did it again, five miles this time, but all my young friends were so tired that they declined the invitation to keep me company. I think that kind of walk in the country is excellent training. I always choose an area with some variety to it, rather than a flat terrain. Every time I have prepared for a fight, I have always found very good spots for walking. Not only does it make you lose weight, it is also excellent for the respiratory system. In fact, I am such a partisan of this form of exercise that, if I weren't a boxer, I might have become a long-distance walker, a rival to Colonel Weston.[2]

We spent several very pleasant days in training camp, in the lovely month of May. One of my first tasks, once we moved in, was to form an orchestra. If I had had to take care of it myself, it would have caused me a lot of trouble. My wife played first violin—she's used to playing the starring role in everything she does—and Kid Cotton knew how to dance a mean jig on the piano keys.

As for me, I had been playing the bass for many years. I chose that instrument because it seemed to suit me better than any other and it's not something that just anybody can handle. I don't claim to be a master of the instrument but I am pleased to be able to say that I can play it to some effect, while many others find it difficult.

I continued doing nothing but road walking for several days and no boxing whatsoever. Some people thought it was mighty risky to go so long without putting on the gloves, but I knew what I was doing. I trusted only myself and didn't ask anyone else's opinion. On the afternoon of May 16, I showed my young friends that I hadn't completely forgotten the art of boxing, by going twenty rounds with Kid Cotton, Marty Cutler, and Denver Jack Geyer, the three heavyweights who had come out from Los Angeles to join us.

At that time, we were a bit preoccupied by the choice of a referee for the upcoming fight. At first, Sam Berger, Jeffries' manager, was determined to choose only men I could not accept and every one I proposed failed to suit him as well. Finally, we agreed on Tex Rickard. Mr. Rickard had never refereed in his life, but I figured that that didn't matter since he knew so much about boxing.

At the same time, Rickard and Gleason realized that they were going to have to abandon their original plan to have the fight take place at the Emeryville racetrack. Some swells who lived in the neighborhood protested against the inconvenience that such a public event would cause them. Consequently, the match had to be moved to San Francisco, where the public wasn't quite so particular; it was said that the authorities would not give permission for the fight easily, but no one paid much attention to the rumor. I didn't worry about it for a second. I knew the bout would take place. Where it took place was a matter of total indifference to me. I let Tex Rickard and Gleason take care of that and I must say they did a mighty good job.

On May 4, Billy Delaney arrived from Harbin Springs and offered to do everything in his power to help me get ready for the fight. He said he had had enough of Jeffries' whole entourage and that he was going to move out to the coast and help me finish up my training, if I wanted him to. No one was more surprised than I to hear Billy approach me in such a friendly way, but I told him I didn't think it would be a very good idea for him to officially move in to my training camp. I did make arrangements for him to come often, though, because I knew there wasn't a man alive who knew Jeffries' tactics as well as he did. I asked him to describe precisely certain specifics of Jeffries' habits in the ring for me. I found Delaney's defection from Jeffries' camp to mine very amusing. I realized that it must be making Jim furious and in fact it was. Anybody would be furious, and with less provocation than that. Jim Corbett went so far as to declare that it was one of the main reasons for Jeffries' defeat. The great man had been in Delaney's care for so long that he was completely dependent on him. And Delaney wasn't an easy man to replace. That's why Corbett's statement doesn't surprise me too much.

It was during this visit that I arranged with Delaney to get Al Kaufmann to join my troop. I chose this rugged young man, above all others, to put the finishing touches on my work. Of all the possible sparring partners in the country, he was certainly the one who seemed best suited to work with a heavyweight boxer; if he makes up his mind to do something about his awkwardness, he will make a fine name for himself in the ring. I needed him to stand up to the hardest of punches and he did exactly that. Billy Delaney agreed with me that Kaufmann was indeed the man for the job, and I wasted no time in hiring him.

Even though everything seemed to be going as well as possible for me, I nonetheless had several causes for concern around this same time. When a man is in training, the least little thing that goes wrong is enough to halt his progress. It is a manager's job to keep all worrisome little interferences out of his boy's sight; but in this case, it was my manager himself who was causing the problems. We hadn't been at Seal Rock House for a week before Little and his wife started becoming so unpleasant that everyone else chose to ignore them altogether. Sig Hart and his wife were so disgusted by Little's behavior that they were just about ready to move out of the hotel. I realized that Little was not a good manager and I showed him the door.

But he refused to leave and started walking around our camp with a revolver in his pocket, saying that he was going to give Sig and me what we were asking for, the first chance he got. That afternoon, he went down to Market Street, repeating the same threats, showing everybody his pistol and yelling that I had robbed him. When I found that out, I went down in my car to find him, with the intention of grabbing the revolver away from him and smashing his face in. The police chief got there just as I did.

"If you make any more noise around here," he told Little, "I'm going to throw you in the dung hole. This thing has gone on long enough. If I ever see you around here again, I'm going to lock you up in the icehouse out on the farm until after the fight."

This surprise attack cooled my manager off a bit and he left without another word that day. But the next day he started in again, making so much noise that I threatened to drop everything then and there and take off with Billy Nolan for the solitude of the area around the lakes, where I could have some peace and quiet. When Rickard and Gleason heard me say that, they were furious.

Now Rickard and Billy Nolan got along just about as well as two fighting cocks. I had a lot of respect for Billy Nolan and he had shown, for his part, that he was a good friend to me. He is a fairly cantankerous fellow and although he doesn't exactly go around looking for fights, he does like to fight as much as any man on earth. He doesn't go around shouting about it. He's not a blowhard, which is more than you can say for some of his enemies.

Although Little did his best to turn my camp into anything but a haven of rest, I didn't give up my work. One day, Dick Adams, one of Jeffries's good friends who had gone to Jeffries' camp to see him work, came to see me too, to get an idea of what I was doing. I knew that every move I made would be faithfully reported back to Jeffries' camp, so I wanted to put on a good show. I took on Al Kaufmann for four rounds; before we began, I told him to hit me as hard as he could. During the sparring session, which was one of the liveliest I've ever had in my life, I wedged my right glove in between Al's arm and his right side. To show my visitor just how weak I was, I lifted Al, all 200 pounds of him, up off the floor and started shaking him until my arm broke free. One of my men was watching Adams as I was doing this. He heard him sigh and saw him shake his head. I found out later that he didn't mention that detail in his report to Jeffries' camp.

Tex Rickard always kept an eye on my speeding. He said he couldn't sleep he was so worried something would happen that would prevent the fight from taking place. He begged me to give up my car for a while; every day, he sent his car, chauffeur at the wheel, around to me. It was a new experience for me to sit on the backseat of a car, but I did it to oblige Tex. Poor man, he had enough to worry about as it was! Between his fear that Governor Gillett would intervene and the impossibility of making everyone happy in his role as referee, those few days were surely the worst of his life.

Twenty-Four

I SET UP CAMP IN RENO

It wasn't until June 17 that we found out that we wouldn't be allowed to fight in California. Rickard and Gleason had endless discussions with Governor Gillett; in the end, he declared that the public morality of the state would be endangered by our exhibition and had us notified that we should clear off. I was genuinely vexed on behalf our two promoters, but I assure you that their long faces were nonetheless a funny sight.

"Cheer up," I told Tex Rickard. "There are plenty of places we can fight."

Tex didn't cheer up.

"But don't you see? " he lamented, "I'm in the process of losing everything I want. I'm headed straight for bankruptcy."

"Listen to what I'm saying," I replied. "Where we fight doesn't matter in the least. One thing is for sure: there's money to be made by everybody."

"I don't know where we're going to go. We're like a band of gypsies," he grumbled.

"What does Jeffries think of all this?" I asked.

"He's crazier than . . . "

"Good. I for one am not. As far as I'm concerned, I hope it'll be in Reno. My wife would very much like to see that town. I think she must have a reason. She's probably thinking how easy it is to get a divorce there."[1]

"I can't believe you're not taking this seriously," said Tex, who looked like he was on the verge of tears.

After a few ups-and-downs, it was finally decided that the bout would be contested in Reno.

We arrived at the station of the famous Nevada divorce city on June 24. An enormous and seemingly friendly crowd was there to greet us. When I stepped down from the train car, I was asked to make a speech. That is one request I rarely refuse. So I stopped on the platform and said something more or less like this:

> Citizens, you have my word that this fight will be on the level. There'll be no sham fighters here. Mr. Jeffries has never put on a fake fight and neither have I. We are going about this thing like sportsmen and when it's over, no one will be able to say that either one of us played anything other than an honest game.

That seemed to please the crowd and they responded with cheers. My sparring partners, Al Kaufmann, Kid Cotton, and Dave Mills were with me and so was my car, so I was feeling very good indeed.

We went right away to a place called Rick's Resort, where we set up my new training camp. I began working on my speed, but with light workouts only for several days until I got used to the altitude. Tom Flanagan, my new manager and sometime trainer, paid a lot of attention to my footwork and every day we worked together.

On the fourth day after we got to this new scene of our exploits, I had a delightful surprise. Governor Dickerson sent me a note telling me that he was going to come to my camp to watch me work out. I immediately notified everybody and told them that the governor had to see us all at our very best; when he arrived, my partners and I were ready and I started in right away on twelve rounds at top speed. When I had finished, I was breathing normally and barely sweating. The governor was very happy with the exhibition.

"There's nothing brutal about this kind of thing," he said, happy as a cat in a dairy, when he saw Kid Cotton hanging on the ropes, opening and closing his big mouth like a carp on a bed of straw, trying to catch the breath that a punch had just knocked out of him.

These words encouraged the Kid; he made a face and rushed at me like a bulldog pup. I landed another punch that sent him into the ropes and the governor enjoyed it even more than the first time. He could barely find words strong enough to express his admiration for our game.

"This is a whole new game for me," he said. "I've gone to lots of prizefights but this is the best battle I've ever seen. This sort of thing leaves a man in better shape when he's finished fighting than when he began."

The Kid just laughed even harder.

I was very happy to have the chance to show the governor what a fight really was, because lots of people have the wrong idea about boxing. I liked the governor very much, too, and I made him aware of that every time I had a chance. He was a young man and had a very straight back, a dark complexion, very sparkling eyes, and curly hair beneath a big Nevada hat. You would never have thought he was a politician; he looked more like a wily businessman. I am sure that I would have become fond of the governor if I had had the chance. I continued working for a little while, to give him an idea of what kind of shape I was really in. I didn't limit myself to defense, I started attacking too. I threw lefts and rights, like a cat batting a toy around, and I jolted my sparring partner like a side of beef.

"No, I have no intention of opposing this bout," the governor said as he left. "I have received your assurance, Mr. Johnson, that this affair is entirely on the up-and-up and that's all I needed."

You can believe that I was very happy indeed to hear Mr. Dickerson say these things, especially since my wife was present; it made me happy to have her hear what a good opinion the governor had of me.[2]

That afternoon, I went down in my car to take a look at the great stadium Tex Rickard had constructed. It had risen from the earth like a puff of smoke but appeared to be very solid despite the haste with which it had been constructed. It had to be solid, because the construction took place under the supervision of the grand jury of Washoe County, who insisted that everything necessary be done to assure the safety of the spectators.

The original plan was designed to hold 17,000 spectators but Rickard had added a new platform that would accommodate an additional 4,000 people. The Reno stationmaster told me that from the three mining towns in the southern part of the state, with a combined population of 2,000 inhabitants, 1,708 requests for tickets had been received.

Twenty-Five

THE END OF MR. J. J. JEFFRIES

The morning of the bout, July 4, 1910, I was feeling rather lazy and didn't get out of bed until 9 A.M. I remember that I would certainly have stayed there even longer if the doctors who were supposed to examine me hadn't arrived at the camp. After their examination, they declared me in good physical condition, which came as a surprise to no one and which I in particular had suspected was the case. The doctors were charming and when the exam was over they asked me to take a ride with them in their car, a type of invitation I rarely if ever refuse. We got into the car and went down into town to take a look at the crowd of people starting to arrive from all over.

When I got back to camp after this very pleasant outing, I ate a good meal, more than I usually eat: four lamb chops, three soft-boiled eggs, several slices of rare meat, and a pot of tea.

At last the big day had arrived! I had never been so happy in my entire long career. I was happy that all the work of getting ready was over, because even though I hadn't tired myself out too much, I don't like being constrained in any way. The thought that made me happiest, though, was that before the sun went down, I would show the world that Jack Johnson was the best man in the ring and that no former champion could take his title away from him.

In my desire to fight my opponent, all the feelings of hate brought on by his earlier behavior toward me had disappeared; I only wanted to win the fight for the supreme position the victory would afford me in the fistic world.

Due to the time it took to get the crowd into the arena, I hopped into the ring an hour later than scheduled. The crowd seemed very happy to see me, above all because that meant that the wait was over. A few minutes later, Jeffries made his appearance and the crowd went wild with enthusiasm. Jeff was wearing old clothes; he had on a soft cap and was chewing gum.

I had donned, for the occasion, a new robe, lined in purple silk. Sam Berger, Jeff's manager, came over to me and asked me to toss a coin to decide which one of us would be in which corner.

"Take whichever corner you like," I told him. "It doesn't matter to me, I'm not picky."

Sam *was* picky, though. He chose the southwest corner, leaving me with the sun in my eyes. Behind Jeff, after his hands had been wrapped, stood Jim Corbett; Billy Delaney took his place behind me. Jeff took off his clothes and appeared in his boxing outfit, red trunks. I took off my robe and appeared in light-blue trunks with an American flag as a belt.

I was not surprised when I saw that the ex-champion forgot the usual formality of the handshake. After all, this was a sign of the fact that there was no friendship between us. I was prepared for this supreme act of impoliteness and it didn't bother me in the slightest. I give you my word of honor, however, that at that moment I felt no personal animosity and that I would have willingly shaken the ex-champion's hand.[1]

"Now you're going to get it, you cowardly nigger!" one of Jeffries' admirers called out from the crowd.

This made me burst out laughing but seemed to excite Jeff, because I saw him make a face in response. At the sound of the bell, I immediately took the offensive. I started off with a good left to the face. Then we clinched and tried to land punches to each other's bodies. But neither of us did much and we circled around the ring until the end of the round.

At the start of the second round, I saw Jeffries coming at me in the old crouching stance that had earned him so much glory in his younger days. Before he could get to me, I threw a left uppercut, which must have shaken the old fellow up. But he took it without batting an eyelash. Then we clinched and wrestled without anyone taking the upper hand.

"Turn off the cameras!" cried the crowd.

When the third round began, I started being less prudent and went back to my old habit of attacking. I feinted a few times to Jeffries' face and eventually we clinched. I landed a couple of punches to his nose and a right-left combination to his neck. Although both punches landed well, Jeffries just looked at me and sneered. My feints hadn't succeeded in forcing the ex-champ to reveal his game plan, assuming he had one.

In the fourth round, Jeffries feinted with his left and I landed a punch on his right eye. I found that very amusing and started kidding Jeffries as much as I could. He landed a few punches to my jaw but I paid little attention to them. Eventually, Tex Rickard got riled up and told us that this was a fight and not a public speaking contest. I laughed and replied that I would never have known it, judging by the punches I was feeling. I saw that Jeffries was throwing low blows and called this fact to his attention. Immediately, Corbett started insulting me, but I didn't care; I just landed two or three good, hard punches on Jeffries. When we went into a clinch, I advised the great man to bring out some of the strength he had been holding back for so long.

In the fifth round, Jeffries went back to his favorite crouching stance.

"I'm going to stand the old gentleman up!" I said to the crowd.

"He's the one who's going to stand you up, you yellow cur!" retorted one of his friends.[2] And the crowd roared. I landed a left to his stomach but I think the ex-champion would have preferred a cup of mint tea. We clinched and I gave him one of my short punches, which split his lip. I followed it up with a couple of blows to the forehead and when we separated, Jeff landed a punch on my forehead, the first serious one he could take credit for.

In the sixth, I started off with a hard punch to the body. Then I landed a left to his cheek and the blood flowed, but he continued to chew his gum as if nothing had happened. I was eager to put an end to that distraction and I unleashed the hardest punch I could on his jaw. At the end of the round, he was bleeding furiously and his hurt eye was getting blacker and blacker. During the rest between rounds, I noticed that he was discussing something with his seconds in his corner and that made me happier than ever.

Jeffries' eye was closed when he came out for the seventh round. As we went into a clinch, I said to him: "Bravo, Jeffries!" Then I landed the most forceful punch I could, a left to the chin, which took away any and all desire he had to continue chewing gum that day. Jim Corbett persisted in needling me but I just laughed.

"Too late to do anything now, Jim," I told him. "Your man is through."

The eighth and ninth rounds were just repetitions of what had come before, with all the advantages on my side. In the tenth round, Jeff used all his energy avoiding me. His seconds were starting to look more and more discouraged and in my corner the joy was increasing at the same rate. Jeff was not a pretty sight to see—he looked exhausted. In a clinch, I worked him over hard with short punches. He tried to land one of his hooks to the body but I blocked it and broke away easily. During this round, my wife, who was sitting in about the sixth row, called out: "Bravo, Jack!" That renewed my courage, so much so that I was beside myself.

The eleventh round was all mine. There was no fight left in my opponent. Jeff was dead tired; try as he might, he couldn't manage to get at me and I was giving him terrible punishment. He was getting weaker by the second and I could see that he wasn't going to last much longer. In the twelfth round, he seemed to make one last effort to hit me. In the thirteenth, his punches were so weak that I didn't even feel them any more. He was having so much trouble lifting his arms, it was as if they were made of lead. He seemed discouraged. When he went back to his corner, he didn't even listen to what his seconds were telling him.

In the fourteenth round, the ex-champion tried to land a punch on my face and I showed him right away how little his punches worried me. He saw that he was just making me laugh and he started to growl. At the end of the round, it was all Jeffries' corner men could do to get him in condition to stand up at the sound of the bell.

The fifteenth round began with a clinch, after Jeff had literally fallen on top of me. I got out from under him and, with a right-left combination to the jaw, sent my man to the canvas. He fell into the ropes on the left side of the ring. The people behind him saw that the moment had come, that he was suffering now what he had made others suffer in the good old days of his youth and power. I turned around and stood in front of the boilermaker, ready with a left hook if he were to get back up. Jim Corbett, who had stood during the entire fight in Jeffries' corner, yelling that I was crazy and that I was in for the fight of my life, lifted his arms to the sky and cried: "Oh, no! Don't hit him, Jack!"

With great difficulty, Jeff stood back up. His jaw was broken, his eyes were closed, and his face was covered with blood. He tried to put his guard back up but I smashed him on the jaw and followed up with two left hooks and he went back down. His doctor and several of his friends jumped into the ring.

"Stop!" they cried. "Don't finish the poor old man off!"

Sam Berger was running in every direction like a madman. Even at this solemn moment, I couldn't help laughing when I looked at Sam. My seconds called out to me, telling me to stay calm. Then Tex Rickard stopped the clock and it was all over.

Jeff buried his head in his hands and muttered: "I was too old to come back."

The last hope of the white race had failed. Since that day, no other has been found to try to replace him.

THE END[3]

EPILOGUE

My homecoming after this sublime and beautiful victory was the greatest event of my career. When the train pulled into the station in Chicago, I found a crowd of more than 5,000 people of my race and nearly as many white people waiting for me. When I stepped down off the Pullman car, it took every bit of strength I had just to make my way to my car, which was parked in front of the station. There were no policemen there that day and yet the crowd was very calm. It gave me great pleasure to walk through the crowd, with cheers ringing out all around me. Once I got behind the wheel, I was in control of the situation. In a splendid takeoff, I left everyone behind me and headed at top speed in the direction of Wabash Avenue, where I knew my mother was anxiously awaiting my arrival.

There I found an entire reception that had been organized in my honor. In front of the house, I first saw a drum major from the black militia band, sumptuously attired and proud as Artaban. As soon as he saw me, he raised his arm and the band struck up the famous song: "Mistah Johnson, Turn Me Loose."

I went into the house. My mother was in the front hall. I grabbed her and picked her up off the ground, so that everybody could see her. She was laughing and crying all at once and everybody was applauding to beat the band. At that exact moment, a friend of the family made his way through the crowd, brandishing a side of bacon. This was a reference to a wire I had sent my mother from Reno: "I'm bringing home the bacon!"

"Here's the bacon!" I shouted to my mother, loud enough for everyone to hear.

"There's no need for it, child," said the good woman. "I made you a fine dinner, John Artha. I cooked it myself and I didn't forget that you like watermelon. I made you some sweets, too, John Artha!"

The crowd demanded a speech. I didn't have one prepared but I went out on the balcony anyway and said a few words, just enough to give a photographer time to take a picture of me.

I went back into the house to feast on the dinner my mother had made for me. I had had good dinners in my life. I take my chef along with me everywhere I go. But the most succulent dishes I have tasted anywhere in the entire world cannot equal the ones my old mother had made for me in her kitchen on Wabash Avenue that day.

I told my sister Lucy that and she said: "I'd be ashamed to admit that if I were you!"

"Oh no, you wouldn't, Miss," I laughed. "Not if you were champion of the world and had just won $168,000 in a fight in Reno."

APPENDIX 1: ADVERTISEMENT FROM *LA VIE AU GRAND AIR* FOR THE SERIALIZED JOHNSON MEMOIR (JANUARY 1911)

A SENSATIONAL PUBLICATION

In our next issue, *La Vie au Grand Air* will begin the sensational publication of the *Memoirs of Jack Johnson*, the world champion of boxing.

We have already told our readers that we would have some surprises for them in the new year. And we are in the habit of keeping our promises. We hope that they will greet with great pleasure the announcement of the story that will begin in the next issue:

The Memoirs of Jack Johnson
World Champion of Boxing

There is no need to point out the great interest of this work. Jack Johnson's fame is well enough established and his career fascinating enough that all sportsmen agree, as they should, on the appeal of these memoirs.

Jack Johnson himself tells his story, from his beginnings to the day he won the world championship title with his victory over Tommy Burns. He tells how he managed to impose himself definitively in the public eye without ever revealing his true worth. Indeed, it is thanks to this strategy that his record includes such a considerable number of bouts, since the promoters had no idea what a remarkable man the nigger was. For ten years now, he has fought all the good boxers there are. Consequently, his memoirs are not of merely personal, but of genuinely historical, interest. In the upcoming issues of *La Vie au Grand Air*, Johnson will in fact recount nothing less than the history of the ring for the past ten years. We hope that our readers will appreciate the great sacrifice that we did not hesitate to make in order to bring them a tale that surpasses all those that have appeared in our columns to date.

PIERRE LAFITTE AND CO.

APPENDIX 2: CHRONOLOGY OF THE LIFE AND BATTLES OF JACK JOHNSON (UP TO 1915)

Note: The events in this chronology are documented facts, in contrast to the Johnson memoir in this volume, which contains both facts and tall tales.

Key to Abbreviations: W= Johnson win (by decision); L= Johnson loss (by decision); D= draw; KO= Johnson win by knockout; TKO=Johnson win by technical knockout; WF= win by foul; LF= loss by foul; LKO= loss by knockout; LTKO= loss by technical knockout; ND= no decision; EX= exhibition. The number following an abbreviation indicates the round in which the fight ended.

1878	March 31: Arthur John Johnson is born (Galveston, Texas).
1895	Summer: First professional fight, against fellow Galveston dock worker John Lee (Johnson wins and earns purse of $50).
1895–1898	Various unofficial bouts, mostly on the docks of Galveston against local opponents.
1896	October: Travels to New York; an unsuccessful attempt to find work as a sparring partner.
1899	March: Moves to Chicago. May 5: Fights "Klondike" (Bill Haines) (LTKO 4) (Chicago). May: In Chicago, works as sparring partner for veteran fighter Frank Childs.

July: In New Haven, CT, helps train featherweight Kid Conroy.
After July: Returns to Galveston.

1900   April 6: Fights Bob White, reputed to be the best boxer in Texas (W 15) (Galveston).
May 1: Fights Jim Scanlon (first known white opponent) (Galveston) (KO 7).
September 8: Hurricane devastates Galveston.
November–December: In Memphis.

1901   February 25: Fights Joe Choynski (Galveston) (LKO 3).
February 25–March 8: Johnson and Choynski in jail in Galveston together, on a charge of having violated the Texas law prohibiting prizefighting.
March–August: In Denver.
August: Moves to California.

1902   March–December: Various fights in California (Klondike, Hank Griffin, Frank Childs et al.).
May 16: Fights Jack Jeffries, brother of Jim Jeffries (San Francisco) (KO 5).

1903   February 3: Fights "Denver" Ed Martin for the "Colored Heavyweight Championship of the World" (Los Angeles) (W 20).
February 3: Defends "Colored Heavyweight Champion of the World" title against Sam McVey (Los Angeles) (W 20).
October 27: Rematch with McVey, again for "Colored Heavyweight" title (Los Angeles) (W 20).

1904   April 22: Third fight with Sam McVey (San Francisco) (KO 20).
Summer: In Philadelphia, plays a few games as first-baseman with all-black Philadelphia Giants.

1905   March 28: Fights Marvin Hart (San Francisco) (L 20).
May 9: Fights Joe Jeannette (Philadelphia) (ND 3).
May 19: Fights Joe Jeannette (Philadelphia) (ND 6).
November 25: Fights Joe Jeannette (Philadelphia) (LF 2).
December 2: Fights Joe Jeannette (Philadelphia) (ND 6).

1906   January 16: Fights Joe Jeannette (New York) (ND 3).
March 14: Fights Joe Jeannette (Baltimore) (W 15).
April 26: Fights Sam Langford (Chelsea, MA) (W 15).
Spring: Takes on Sam Fitzpatrick and Alec McLean as managers.

September 20: Fights Joe Jeannette (Philadelphia) (ND 6).

November 26: Fights Joe Jeannette (Portland, ME) (D 10).

December 9: Fights Joe Jeannette (New York) (W 3).

1907   January 24: With McLean, arrives in Sydney, Australia.

Late January–early March: Fights a series of exhibition bouts in Australia.

February 19: Fights Australian Peter Felix for "Colored Heavyweight Championship of the World" (Sydney) (KO 1).

March 18: Arrested for assaulting McLean.

April 24: Sails for America.

May 18: Arrives in San Francisco.

July 17: Fights Bob Fitzsimmons (Philadelphia) (KO 2).

August: Begins liaison with Hattie McClay.

November 2: Fights "Fireman" Jim Flynn (San Francisco) (KO 11).

1908   January 3: Fights Joe Jeannette (New York) (D 3).

Spring–summer: In London, in pursuit of Tommy Burns.

June: In Paris, in pursuit of Tommy Burns.

October: Arrives in Australia.

December 26: Fights Tommy Burns for Heavyweight Championship of the World (Sydney) (W 14) (becomes first black heavyweight champion of the world).

1909   March 9: Arrives back in North America.

Spring: Takes on George Little as manager.

April: Begins liaison with Belle Schreiber.

May 19: Defends title against "Philadelphia" Jack O'Brien (Philadelphia) (ND 6).

June 30: Defends title against Tony Ross (Philadelphia) (ND 6).

September 9: Defends title against Al Kaufmann (San Francisco) (ND 10).

October 16: Defends title against Stanley Ketchel (Colma, CA) (KO 12).

November 30: Signs for fight with Jim Jeffries (promoted by Tex Rickard and Jack Gleason).

Date unspecified: Buys a house for his mother, "Tiny" Johnson, in Chicago (3344 South Wabash).

1910   April 30–June: In training for Jeffries fight at Seal Rock House (San Francisco).

June 6: Fires manager George Little.

June 26: Arrives in Reno for Jeffries fight.

July 4: Defends title against Jim Jeffries (Reno, NV) (KO 15).

July 4: News of Johnson's victory sparks rioting in cities across the country, resulting in "at least eleven and perhaps as many as twenty-six" deaths (Ward, p. 217).

July 7: Triumphant homecoming in Chicago.

October 25: Races legendary racecar driver Barney Oldfield (Sheepshead Bay, Brooklyn).

1911   January 18: Marries Etta Terry Duryea in Pittsburgh.

January 21–May 20: French sporting periodical, *La Vie au Grand Air*, publishes "Ma Vie et mes combats," memoirs of Jack Johnson, in weekly instalments.

Mid–June: Arrives in England (with Etta).

Late August–September 23: In Paris (with Etta); boxes a series of exhibition bouts with Georges Carpentier at "Magic City."

October 2: Scheduled fight with British heavyweight champion "Bombardier" Billy Wells, in London (cancelled on order of Home Secretary Winston Churchill).

December 22: Arrives back in New York.

1912   July 4: Defends title against "Fireman" Jim Flynn (Las Vegas, NM) (WF 9).

July 10: Grand opening of the *Café de Champion* in Chicago (241 W 31st St.).

September 12: Etta Terry Duryea Johnson dies of a self-inflicted gunshot wound.

Early October: Appears in public with Lucille Cameron on his arm.

October 30: Chicago authorities close down the *Café de Champion*.

November 7: Arrested for violation of the Mann Act (forbidding the transportation of women across state or national borders "for the purpose of prostitution or debauchery, or for any other immoral purposes"); is released on bail a week later.

December 3: Marries Lucille Cameron in Chicago.

1913   May 5: *United States v. John Arthur Johnson* begins.

May 13: Convicted on all counts.

June 4: Sentenced to one year and one day in the penitentiary and fined $1,000.

June 24: Flees to Canada.

June 29: Leaves Montreal for Le Havre.

July–August 24: In Paris.

August 24: Arrives in England.

October–December: In Paris.

October: Stripped of his title by the *Fédération Française de Boxe* (the International Boxing Union declines to follow suit).

December 19: Defends title against "Battling" Jim Johnson (Paris) (D 10).

1914   Date unspecified: *Mes Combats*, a book based on but not identical to the 1911 *Vie au Grand Air* series published in Paris by Pierre Lafitte et Cie.

June 27: Defends title against Frank Moran (Paris) (W 20) (refereed by Georges Carpentier).

July: In St. Petersburg.

August 1: War is declared; flees St. Petersburg for London, by way of Paris.

December: Leaves England for Buenos Aires.

1915   January: In Buenos Aires.

February 15: Arrives in Cuba.

April 3: Fights Sam McVey (Havana) (EX 6).

April 5: Defends title against Jess Willard (Havana) (LKO 26).

Sources: Randy Roberts, *Papa Jack: Jack Johnson and the Era of White Hopes* (New York: The Free Press, 1983); Geoffrey Ward, *Unforgivable Blackness: The Rise and Fall of Jack Johnson* (New York: Knopf, 2004); and http://www.cyberboxingzone.com/boxing/jjohn.htm.

NOTES

PREFACE

1. *La Vie au Grand Air*, XIX (644–661) (January 21–May 20, 1911).

CHAPTER 4

1. In the 1911 French text, the filly's name is given as "Mlle. Suzon" but this extremely French name seems improbable, given the context. I am guessing that the name is in fact a translation from the English on the part of whoever translated and transcribed Johnson's words, hence my decision to use "Miss Susie."

CHAPTER 5

1. Johnson biographer Geoffrey Ward provides a description of this first professional fight, against fellow dockworker John "Must Have It" Lee. See Geoffrey Ward, *Unforgivable Blackness: The Rise and Fall of Jack Johnson* (New York: Knopf, 2004), pp. 13–14.
2. Geoffrey Ward, *Unforgivable Blackness*, p. 29, reports that this was one of Johnson's favorite self-mythologizing anecdotes and that there is variation among the different versions.

CHAPTER 8

1. [Note in 1911 text] The match that pitted Jimmy Britt and Joe Gans against each other, in San Francisco, was not on the level. Joe Gans himself told the story in

the confessions he published before he fought Battling Nelson. He swore he would never again use the less-than-sportsmanlike tactic that his opponents had made him agree to in order to get fights.

2. Note that Johnson says that he knocked out five men in 1902, but only names four (each of whom he KO'd once that year).

CHAPTER 10

1. Johnson's fight with Jack Munroe took place on June 26, 1905. It is true that Munroe had lasted four rounds in an exhibition against Jeffries (December 19, 1902). Johnson fails to mention, however, that Munroe had also been knocked out by Jeffries in his bid for Jeffries' title on August 26, 1904. See http://www.cyberboxingzone.com, for Jeffries' official record.

CHAPTER 11

1. The 1911 text does not identify the source of this or the other newspaper clipping quoted below (the 1914 version does not include them at all).

CHAPTER 15

1. Tommy Burns' real name was indeed Noah Brusso and he was indeed Canadian. It seems, however, that he was not Jewish. One can only speculate as to the possible sources of, and motivations for, Johnson's assertion.

2. See note above, on Johnson's assertion that Burns/Brusso was Jewish.

CHAPTER 16

1. There is an interesting discrepancy between the 1911 and 1914 versions here: In the earlier version, Johnson says Burns refuses to quit because he is a "courageous little guy" (*courageux petit gars*), while in the later one, his refusal is interpreted as "stubborn" (*entêté*). If Johnson did in fact participate in the 1914 revision of the text, he would seem to have become more rather than less cynical vis-à-vis Burns with the passage of time. I have chosen to go with the later version.

2. This number comes from the 1911 text; in the 1914 version it is $1,000. In spite of the fact that the later version is in some ways a correction of its predecessor, I have gone with the earlier version in this case simply because it seems more mathematically likely.

3. The term "winnings" here (*gains* in the French) seems to be a reference to the money Johnson won betting on himself. If his share of the gate was indeed $15,000 (see note above) and his purse, as he says earlier, $5,000, his gambling profit would have been something along the lines of $5,000, at least according to this version of the story.

CHAPTER 17

1. No wedding, simple or otherwise, took place in Australia. When Jack Johnson married Etta Duryea in Chicago, on January 18, 1911 (two years after the wedding alleged here would have taken place), he stated that he had always been single and that indeed appears to have been the case. There had been, however, a series of women prior to this first marriage who traveled with him using the name "Mrs. Jack Johnson." One of them, the woman to whom he refers here, was Hattie McClay, who was on board ship with Johnson on his return from Australia and whom Johnson did introduce to reporters upon arrival in Vancouver as his wife ("the former Nellie O'Brian of Philadelphia"). On Johnson and McClay's presenting themselves as a married couple to reporters in Vancouver, see Ward, *Unforgivable Blackness*, pp. 138–139; on Johnson's marriage to Etta Duryea, see pp. 254–255.

CHAPTER 19

1. [Note in both 1911 and 1914 texts] Jack Johnson forgets to mention here that he was in fact knocked down by one of Ketchel's rights. Since Joe Choynski, only two men, Ketchel and Sam Langford, have had the honor of sending the world champion to the canvas.

CHAPTER 20

1. This passage comes directly from Jeffries' autobiography: James Jackson Jeffries, *My Life and Battles: The World Champion* (New York: Ringside, 1910), p. 55. In both versions of the Johnson text, the passage appears in French translation only. Significantly, whoever did the translation chose to omit and/or disregard Jeffries' racist renderings of Johnson's speech. For example, the ignorant-sounding "Dear Misto Jeffries [. . .] I ain't no cellar fighter. I want to fight in public, with a referee. I don't want to fight in no cellar" becomes the dignified "I fight in a ring, not in a cellar; before an audience, not in secret" (*Je combats sur un ring, et non dans une cave; devant le public, et non en secret*).

There are also slight changes in the content of the anecdote: the original Jeffries text has Johnson affirming and reaffirming his desire to fight Jeffries ("Ah really want to fight yo', Misto Jeff" [. . .] "I shore do"), while the French translation has Johnson responding to Jeffries' reproaches by saying, "You really want to fight me too, Mister Jeff" (*Ah vraiment, vous désirez me combattre aussi, M. Jeff*).

In Jeffries' text, he openly insults Johnson, saying he's "not even a four-flush" but rather a "three-flush." This is omitted altogether in the French version. The motivation behind these changes is not entirely clear. Johnson does come off better in the French, but, ironically, so does Jeffries, since his overt racism and arrogance are softened.

2. Jeffries, *My Life and Battles*, p. 56. In contrast to the previous citation from the Jeffries autobiography, the French version matches the original English more or less exactly in this case.

CHAPTER 21

1. The 1914 text has this as January 1910, clearly a mistake, since the pressure on Jeffries to fight Johnson began immediately after Johnson won the title from Burns in December 1908. (The 1911 text says "January of last year," suggesting that the text published in 1911 was written in 1910).

CHAPTER 23

1. There is a curious discrepancy between the two versions here. In the 1911 version, Johnson says that he "waited until May 9 to get to work." In the 1914 version, he says that he didn't "begin to think of [training] until May 4." I've chosen to use the 1911 version, simply because training is clearly more important than thinking about training.

2. [Note in 1911 text] Weston, who was never a colonel in his life, is famous for having crossed the United States, from San Francisco to New York, on foot.

CHAPTER 24

1. Whether he actually said it at the time or invented it for his memoir, this joking comment is odd, since Johnson was not in fact married at all in the summer of 1910 and wouldn't be for another six months. On Johnson's real and pretend marriages, and the chronology thereof, see Chapter 17, note 1, above.

2. In both French texts, the governor is erroneously referred to as "Dickinson." Whether the mistake was Johnson's or that of the French translator/transcriber of his memoir is anyone's guess. Denver S. Dickerson was governor of Nevada from 1908 to 1910. In a curious coincidence, Johnson would cross paths again with Dickerson, long after the writing of this memoir and in a context very different from the one described here. At the time of Johnson's incarceration in Leavenworth (1920–1921) on the infamously trumped-up Mann Act conviction, Dickerson was the superintendent of prisons and president of the parole board. According to Geoffrey Ward, who details Johnson's time in prison, Dickerson may or may not have been directly responsible for the relatively easy time Johnson had in Leavenworth. Ward quotes Johnson's 1927 autobiography, in which he says that Dickerson was "a staunch friend and adviser" during his entire time behind bars. See Ward, *Unforgivable Blackness*, pp. 405–406, and Jack Johnson, *Jack Johnson: In the Ring and Out* (New York: Citadel Press, 1992), pp. 127–128.

CHAPTER 25

1. Ward, *Unforgivable Blackness*, p. 207, says: "Rickard [. . .] announced that there would be no traditional handshake, no posing for the cameras; the white man had refused to take part." Other biographers and at least one contemporary account say

that the two fighters had mutually agreed ahead of time not to shake. See Randy Roberts, *Papa Jack: Jack Johnson and the Era of White Hopes* (New York: The Free Press, 1983), p. 104 and p. 244, note 50. *Jack Johnson: In the Ring and Out* makes no mention of there having been no handshake.

2. Ward, based on a contemporary account in the *New York Times*, reports that this exchange took place in the ninth round (not the fifth, as Johnson would have it here) and that the Jeffries fan in fact yelled, "He'll straighten *you* up, Nigger!" See Ward, *Unforgivable Blackness*, p. 209.

3. The 1914 text ends here. The 1911 text concludes with a short final chapter, a sort of postscriptum, chronicling Johnson's homecoming after the Jeffries fight. I have chosen to use that as an epilogue.

About the Author

CHRISTOPHER RIVERS is Professor of French at Mount Holyoke College. He is the author of *Face Value: Physiognomical Thought in Lavater, Marivaux, Balzac, Gautier and Zola* (1994) as well as a number of articles on eighteenth- and nineteenth-century French literature. He is also the translator and editor of Adophe Belot's 1870 novel, *Mademoiselle Giraud, ma femme* (2002). He is currently working on a cultural biography of the great French boxer Georges Carpentier.

JACK JOHNSON was the first African-American heavyweight champion of the world and a seminal and iconic figure in the history of race in America.